NATURE FOR THE VERY YOUNG

A Handbook of Indoor and Outdoor Activities

Marcia Bowden

Illustrated by *Marilyn Rishel*

WILEY

John Wiley & Sons, Inc.
New York • Chichester • Brisbane • Toronto • Singapore

To the memory of
Grandma Mary
who always said,

"Let's go for a walk."

Copyright © 1989 by John Wiley & Sons, Inc.

Library of Congress Cataloging-in-Publication Data

Bowden, Marcia.
  Nature for the very young: A handbook of indoor and outdoor activities

  Bibliography: p. 225
  1. Nature study.   2. Education, Preschool.   I. Title.
II. Series.
LB1140.5.S35B68   1989   372.3'57   88-33747
ISBN 0-471-50975-2
ISBN 0-471-62084-X (pbk.)

Printed in the United States of America
89 90 10 9 8 7 6 5 4 3 2 1

Preface

Why study nature with preschoolers? A director of an environmental association once asked me, "What on earth do you do with those little ones anyway?" He couldn't imagine anything more than glorified babysitting.

But the truth is that early childhood is the perfect time to introduce environmental education. Nature study capitalizes on young children's characteristics: it wants them to touch, to move actively, to ask questions. In short, learning about nature requires the active use of all the senses, and preschoolers just do that naturally. There is never a problem with motivation; children enjoy learning about the outdoor world around them. It is an activity which engages children's inclinations to run, to touch, to explore. It is a very concrete experience. Young children can use all their senses to explore the natural world. It is a positive experience; no one will say, "Don't touch that dandelion."

The demand for early childhood experiences is increasing. Parents are not only taking their children to nursery schools and day-care centers, but also to nature centers. They are insisting on more and more organized activities for younger and younger children. To meet this demand, nature centers are offering hours for preschoolers. Nature centers and preschools alike can use nature activities, satisfying this demand as well as providing experiences that allow children the freedom to be children.

As mentioned above, nature study is ideal for the school situation. There is never a problem with motivation. In fact, things such as ants, which don't appeal to most adults (let alone interest them), fascinate small children. Children have an innate curiosity about their world, an inquisitiveness that is just waiting for the teacher to develop.

Nature study is an experience that children can have at school and repeat at home. It provides a much needed continuity of learning that links school and home. Children learn methods of discovery at school and continue to discover at home. Nature study is an activity that weans the learner from the teacher.

Because learning about nature fascinates all young children, it is a good conduit for other learning tasks, such as readiness activities. An interest in birds, for example, can lead a child through left-to-right progression activities with enjoyment (see the section on chickadees, page 45).

The basic ingredients of nature study are both free and accessible. Even the city child can find a patch of sand filled with ants, a crack in the sidewalk with a weed sprouting out of it, a vacant lot nearby. You don't have to spend money. You don't have to go anywhere.

These are the down-to-earth reasons why I advocate nature study for young children.

The philosophical reasons are harder to pin down. They have to do with values and enrichment of life. By studying the natural world around them, children gain an appreciation of that world. They learn that we are part of that world. They gain a respect for other living things. Also, it is better for a child to be an active participant in that natural world rather than a passive observer. These reasons are not new. Anna Comstock, writing in 1911, said:

> Out-of-door life takes the child afield and keeps him in the open air, which not only helps him physically and occupies his mind with sane subjects, but keeps him out of mischief.

Finally, kids today are often pseudosophisticated, world-weary beyond their years. Too much is expected of them emotionally, and not enough creatively. Nature study allows children to be children. They are free to do childlike things such as exclaim, wonder, and explore.

Acknowledgments

This book is the direct result of children's curiosity. We express our gratitude to all those children in nature centers, libraries, day-care centers, nursery schools, kindergartens, and schools who led us through these lessons.

In particular, we wish to thank our children:

Patience whose fascination with rocks at age two started it all;

Andy who marvels at each new caterpillar he finds;

April who enjoys making things with nature;

Alethe who discovers what others miss.

Our appreciation extends to all the directors of nature centers, nursery schools, Head Start Programs, libraries, and schools who let the "milkweed ladies" in.

We sincerely thank our original editor, Mary Kennan, of Dodd, Mead Publishers and David Sobel, our editor at John Wiley & Sons, whose persistence brought all this to fruition. We are indebted to Lila M. Gardner of Spectrum Publisher Services who skillfully assembled these pages.

To James and Bill, our love and thanks for their continuing encouragement.

Marcia Bowden
Maple Rock

Marilyn Rishel
Orchard Hill

Contents

A Walk for Thinking

It's quiet in the meadow
When we go for a walk
And mother doesn't hear me
Or answer when I talk.

She says it's a walk for thinking
Or to watch the summer sky
Or to look for ladyslippers
Or hear the wild geese cry

But I like to jabber
And tell her about things
Like sourgrass and bluebirds
And a fairy child with wings

And how the Johnny-jump-ups
Have faces and can see.
I ask her where the moon is now
But she doesn't answer me.

But when we're walking home again
And evening shadows fall
I can put my hand in hers
And she hears me after all.

By Nancy Dingman Watson from
*Blueberries Lavender: Songs
of the Farmer's Children*

INTRODUCTION

This book is a compilation of the ideas and activities I have developed over the years. I began by using them with my own children and later with groups of children at nature centers, schools, and libraries. I have also presented these activities at both parent and teacher workshops. These ideas have been field tested (literally!) over and over. They work in both a parent-child relationship and a teacher-student situation.

I live in New England. My students and I are surrounded by stone walls, gray squirrels, and white pines. Obviously, the nature activities we engage in arise from our unique environment. But don't let these specifics stop you. Use these ideas as a springboard for forming your own lessons. Don't have stone walls? Explore the chain-link fence or the fence row. Don't have gray squirrels? Observe the fox squirrel. No white pines with their five-needle bundles to teach the number five? Then how about using the scrub pine with its two-needle bundles to teach the number two!

Delve into the natural environment of your region. See its connection with small children. Incorporate it with readiness activities.

I have observed many nature center preschool hours that go something like this: Observe a captured ferret; cut open an apple sideways to see the "flower" inside; then go on a nature walk. While all this is fun for young children, it is also confusing. They come away with a variety of unrelated sensations and no coherent whole.

As mentioned above, the best way for children to learn is to engage all their senses. Paradoxically, they also need to learn to focus their scattered attention. In an attempt to combine these two attributes, each lesson in this book develops one topic, which encourages the child to attend, to focus. At the same time, each lesson consists of a variety of activities that engage several senses—all centered, however, around that one topic.

The goal is to learn about a particular habitat in all its seasonal changes. This habitat can be the schoolyard, a nearby town park or vacant city lot, or a field at a nature center. Children learn the whole by examining the parts. By year's end, they have experienced this one habitat in all its seasonal changes. They have lived it! They have gained an idea of which plants and animals live in that habitat, as well as a glimmer of the interrelationships between those plants and animals.

The activities in this book are structured. There are definite activities, definite guidelines, definite topics. This is not a book that simply urges "go outside and groove"—although I strongly urge you to do that, too. There is a time to go out and lie on the grass, to run through the park, to *be* outside. I assume that this is already part of your daily routine with the children. These lessons are a supplement, which, hopefully, will enhance those free times.

O.K. You are now convinced that you should take the children outside and explore. The thought of thirty three-year-olds outside can be overwhelming. How do you start?

First, stress that nature study time is not recess. This is not a time to yell and run with wild abandon. It is a time to learn. This behavior may take a while to learn, so the first few trips outside should be short. Gradually increase the time outside as the children increase their ability to attend. The lessons in this book are suggestions. Use parts of them as your students' attention requires, perhaps stretching them out over several days, or even weeks.

Children outdoors are enthusiastic, to put it mildly. The trick is to encourage this enthusiasm without letting it dissolve into chaos. Start with those short visits outside, having the children attend to one topic. The traditional nature walk, with the adult at the head of a long string of children, just does not work with young children. The child at the end of the line is always missing out; the child at the beginning is ready to move on.

During nature walks, young children's attention is difficult to focus. They see something interesting along the way, get distracted, and, naturally, want to run to that object. So, go to one spot and explore the topic for the day there. Make sure there is enough of the topic (dandelions, ants, and such) for everyone to examine. If this is impossible (for example, if there is only one oak tree), take out small groups so that each child can see and touch easily without having to wait. They cannot wait! It doesn't matter how patiently you explain, "Oh, you'll get your turn. I'll make sure everyone can see." They still crowd and push and whine, "Teacher, teacher, I can't see."

Children like to pick up stuff: flowers, stones, and acorns all find their way into the hands of preschoolers. At a nature center with a strict no-pick policy, this can create some problems. Perhaps allowing the child to pick something to hold (maybe a dandelion) will satisfy that "pick urge." Begin introducing plants that are endangered and explain simply that we do not pick these because there just are not enough. Gradually, as children learn more about their natural world, they come to see that that old, abandoned nest, or even that little twig, has a use and is best left alone.

Day-care centers and nursery schools should scout out the site ahead of time for dangerous or annoying conditions, such as scattered, broken glass, dog droppings, or poison ivy. Make sure your explorations are on your property or public property. If not, get permission from the property owner.

When you get to the site, some children are so excited that they just run. You may want to start by having them run (or hop, or skip) to a designated tree, to a chain-link fence, or to a rock. This accomplishes two results: that initial frantic energy is dissipated, and by having them run to designated areas, they are learning the boundaries, the permitted space of exploration.

If you are lucky enough to have aides, review with them *in advance* the boundaries and the behavior expectations so that the children are not getting conflicting requests. If you do use aides or parent volunteers, make it clear that they are not to group together and talk. At nature center preschool hours, do not let a parent come along unless all the parents are coming. If one parent comes along, then halfway through the hour, other children start wanting their parents. Many children act babyish when Mom or Dad is along. Also, Mom or Dad gets interested in the topic and starts asking natural history questions, unintentionally monopolizing the teacher-naturalist's time.

Nature centers should plan some parent-child explorations, encourage adults to come to adult programs at the center, and pass out brief information sheets on natural history that describe what went on that day. Suggest parent-child activities and encourage parents to take natural history walks with their children.

If children do get restless during the lesson, or just plain need to move, incorporate a movement activity into the lesson. Be sure to do so before they get restless and you've lost them. Ask such questions as "Can you hop like a rabbit?" or play a dramatic singing game such as "Oats and Beans and Barley," a traditional tune found in folk song books (see Resources).

The lessons in this book are for both outdoor and indoor sessions. Nature centers can use the introductory indoor sessions to effective advantage. Because you don't see the children often, you need to develop some continuity. Use this time to set up some routine activities that are performed at every session. This gives the children time to settle down, to become comfortable in this new setting. These activities will come to signal to the children that "nature-study time" is here. It cues the children as to what to expect and what behavior is expected of them.

Spend time going over everyone's name. Perhaps you'll want to make name tags. Children do fiddle with them, and some people feel they are better off without them. Make sure the children know your name; have them say it. Give them time to get to know each other. Often, this is their only social experience, and it is just as important to them as the lesson. Knowing the children's names increases their self-esteem. It may also prove crucial when one child has darted away and you need to get her back immediately when you're outside.

Allow enough time for putting on and taking off coats, hats, and mittens. Encourage parents, either through a letter home, or in person, to have the children dress appropriately for the weather. There is nothing so miserable as an uncomfortable child. If the day's activities are different than usual—let's say you're going to a wet spot to look at skunk cabbage hoods—then be sure to give parents advance notice of the required clothing, such as boots.

Preschoolers have no tolerance for lectures. Do as little talking as possible. The natural history information provided in this book is for your background, to help you answer questions. Do not use it to develop lectures on the subject; you'd be wasting your breath. This does not mean that you do not provide information. You do: by answering questions, by using flannel board stories, by encouraging dramatic play.

Determine what vocabulary, if any, you want the children to learn that day. Use that word frequently throughout the day in context. Do not use similes, comparisons, or other figures of speech. Children think very literally. They will remember the simile and not the fact—and it is very difficult to unlearn material.

Many of the following lessons deal with generalities, for example, frogs are green; toads are brown. That's O.K. As children get older, they will easily incorporate exceptions to their basic store of knowledge.

With the exception of the violet lesson on page 175, we have omitted suggestions for eating wild foods. Unquestionably, there are many wonderful outdoor treats, and it has been a real exercise in restraint not to mention them. However, unsupervised young children at home can easily court disaster by "eating red berries just like we did at school." Not wanting to ignore the sense of taste, however, we have included recipes with conventional ingredients, for example, toad pretzels.

The purpose of this book is twofold.

First, it provides a variety of easy to prepare lesson plans. Many of them are large enough to photocopy—and you have an instant lesson! Most of the teaching aids should be mounted on heavy cardboard and laminated with clear adhesive. I suggest you find access to a copier with enlargement capabilities so that you can use all of the artwork as teaching tools.

Nature magazines are invaluable for their pictures as well as their articles. The ones I use most frequently are published by the National Wildlife Federation: *Your Big Backyard, Ranger Rick,* and *National Wildlife* magazine. Two useful Canadian publications are *Owl* and *Chickadee.* (See Resources for further information.)

When you use the pictures, try to take the time to mount them on construction paper and laminate them. They will last much longer.

Collect as many back issues as you can. Duplicate copies provide identical pictures for many of the activities described in the following lessons.

Secondly, we hope that some of our enthusiasm for nature study will inspire you to develop your own nature lessons. Here are some guidelines to help you along:

First and foremost, watch children. Develop your lessons around their natural tendencies. They want to touch everything. They are constantly moving. See these as positive characteristics, as ways to satisfy their insatiable curiosity.

Use our lessons as an incentive for developing lessons for your own particular environment. Don't have snow? How about rain? No stone walls? What's growing by the chain-link fence?

- Explore your entire habitat. Use all your senses. What do you see? Look up and down. Listen, feel. Lie down on your back and look up. Lie on your stomach and look down. Explore as a child does. Feel, sift through

dirt, grass. Get on your knees to get a three-year-old's visual perspective. Close your eyes. Be very still for several minutes. Record what you hear. Choose *one* natural object that interests you. Can you identify it? Observe it closely for as long as possible. Write down all your observations.
- Research that object. Use libraries and the local nature center.
- Choose one aspect of that object that you want to stress. For example, while studying pine trees, I was fascinated with the concept of five needles to a bundle, and the concept of five became the basis of my lesson.
- Tie this in with a readiness skill you wish to stress.
- Above all, keep it simple!

For reference material, see the list of Resources for magazines and books. Your local library is invaluable. Through the wonders of interlibrary loan, they can get almost anything. Also, many libraries are waiting for someone to cart away their back issues of *Ranger Rick* just for the asking.

Although you can certainly do without the following two items, I have found them helpful:

Plastic hand lenses—obtainable from Museum Products (see Resources). Very small children, even two-year-olds, can use hand lenses, but they must be taught how. Most children hold the hand lens right up to one eye and peer through it. Others are more successful holding it about a foot away from their eyes. Determine this for each child. Then have the children look at their fingerprints. Go to each child to make sure they are seeing them. Ask, "What happens when we use the hand lens? Yes, it makes things bigger." Practice using the hand lens on common objects in the room before using it outside.

Autoharp—easy to play. Just push a button and strum the strings. Watch the wide eyes and spreading grins—instant attention! And sing! Three-year-olds certainly don't care what your voice sounds like. So don't be bashful. Make up songs to familiar tunes. Or, even easier, repeat one sentence over and over. (See the snow lesson on page 79 for my chart buster, "What Color Is the Snow on the Ground?")

Music and nature and children—a magical combination.

AUTUMN

Time
of
Preparation

The days of summer stretch on endlessly. In late July, when heat waves linger and cicadas shrill at noon, we wonder, "Will it ever end?"

Winter seems even longer. By February, when the delight in snow has melted and the cold is a matter of endurance, we wonder, "Will it ever end?"

Do you remember a similar day in late October when you've said, "Oh brother, when will autumn ever end?"

No?

There is no mid-autumn, says Edwin Way Teale, because this is a season of change. Every single day is different from the one before it. These changes reflect preparation. For during this transitional time, all of nature is preparing for winter survival. Birds, plants, animals, and insects are getting ready. Some escape winter by migrating or hibernating. Others cope.

As sunlight hours diminish and cold seeps in, insect and plant populations drop. Plants hasten to scatter their final seeds to ensure new growth in spring. Insects get into position to overwinter in one phase of their life cycle. Many birds fly south for a more adequate food supply. Mammals eat to gain body fat, and some store food here and there. Deciduous trees, in an effort to avoid the death-dealing moisture loss of winter, drop their leaves and batten down for survival.

With such frantic activity, no wonder each day is different. This sense of change, of urgency, of *Things Going On!* provides an exciting season of discovery for children.

At the same time, they, too, must prepare. These preparations, or readiness activities, lead to a different kind of survival: that of reading and comprehension. The lessons that follow combine reading readiness activities with autumn explorations.

HABITAT

Habitat is probably one of the most difficult words for children to understand. I don't know why; I think it's our fault. We tend to explain too much when defining habitat. In simplest terms, a habitat is a place where an animal or plant lives. To extend that definition a little further, that place has certain characteristics, which in combination make it possible for a particular animal or plant to live there.

A pond is an example of one habitat. Certain animals live near the pond (raccoons) because it provides a source of water. Certain insects (dragonflies) are found hovering over the pond as they lay their eggs. Certain birds (humming-

birds) build their nests over the water. Certain plants (cat-tails) grow at the pond's edge. Other animals and plants cannot live in a pond habitat. You won't see a whale there, for example.

Habitat is one of the most important ecological concepts to understand in today's world. The destruction of particular habitats is endangering entire species. As swamps are filled to make room for housing and bamboo forests are cut to make room for fields, these habitats with their particular combinations of food and shelter for particular animals are lost.

Not that you should even consider discussing the ecological implications of habitat destruction with small children. However, now *is* the time for laying the groundwork for eventual understanding of these problems.

Young children instinctively respond to the concept of habitat. Physically, they are very attuned to their surroundings, to their own habitats. They often react dramatically with all their senses to changes in habitat. The suburban four-year-old, for example, confidently goes off to nursery school. She knows not to run into the street. She shows interest in passing traffic but does not fear it. She handles herself well in crowds at shopping malls. In contrast, her visiting rural cousin is shy when meeting children in a school setting, has no sense of traffic safety, and is fearful in large crowds.

On the other hand, the rural child scrambles with ease over rocks, hops across stones in the brook, ducks the sumac branches on the meadow's edge. The suburban child, on a country visit, stumbles on the rocks, gets caught in the green briar, and is whapped in the face with a wayward branch. Children have a sense of their own habitat and often do not feel comfortable when plunked into a new one.

Children respond physically to different natural habitats. Take children to a field and watch as they automatically run and leap. First they skirt the edge, running. Then they make a pell-mell dash through the center and throw themselves onto the ground. They leap after grasshoppers, all the while shouting exuberantly. Children turn their faces to the sun's warmth and smile. Children do not fear meadows; they revel in them.

I know naturalists who prefer the forest to the field because "you can't control the kids in the field." I say, that's the field's fault! It invites this leaping, abandoned behavior. Maybe that's O.K. Maybe an hour of field running is more than equal to all our well-planned habitat lessons.

Go into a forest. While the children still chatter, their voices are lower, they crowd more closely around the adult. They keep their eyes to the ground. Some children may even be fearful and talk of "bears in the woods."

The children's behavior reflects the habitat. Look at the animals of the field: the rabbits, the grasshoppers, the butterflies. See how they hop and fly with (to our eyes) abandon. Grasses, like the children, turn their faces to the sun and absorb the warmth with a grin. Then consider the animals of the forest: the sowbugs and salamanders, which creep quietly under logs. Forest mammals move stealthily; indeed, they are not often seen. The trees rise ever upward with dignity.

The best way to learn habitat is to live it. Throughout the year, encourage the children to explore the schoolyard or nature-center trails. Bit by bit, they will come to know the whole.

CLASSIFICATION SKILLS

One type of naturalist's habitat lesson goes something like this: "O.K., kids, today we're gonna learn about *habitat*. We will be looking at a field, a forest, and a stream today. You are to investigate each of these habitats thoroughly. In your investigations, include air and soil temperatures as well as an inventory for all plants and animals. Determine the relationships between these plants and animals and then fill out these charts I'm handing out. Oh yes, here are your pencils and backboards. When you're finished, we'll meet back at the Nature Hut to compare and contrast these three varying *habitats*."

Needless to say, this approach does not exactly work with young children. So, start with what they know.

If you are in a school situation that meets on a frequent basis, begin with a unit about the neighborhood. Take a series of walks with the children around the immediate neighborhood. Start with short trips, gradually lengthening them. If possible, take the school bus or van for a ride around your city or town. Visit such places as a school, a fire station, the city hall, an apartment house, a single dwelling, a playground, a store, a library, a police station, and a church. During block play, encourage the children to recreate the neighborhood. Discuss the shapes, textures, and materials of the buildings. Stress the functions of each building. Listen to neighborhood sounds: jackhammers, people's voices, traffic, horns, sirens, dogs barking. Most importantly, talk about the people of the neighborhood and how each contributes in some way to that neighborhood.

In a nature-center setting where you haven't the time to develop a lengthy unit, begin the session by reading a picture book about neighborhoods. Discuss the children's neighborhood. Ask who lives next door, what business people and stores are around. Are there people who deliver mail or fuel oil, or read the meter? Sing "Sesame Street's" song "The People in Your Neighborhood."

When children comprehend "neighborhood," start the habitat lesson by holding up a picture of a grasshopper (or, even better, a live one) and say, "Today we are going to visit the neighborhood of this grasshopper." As the lesson progresses, use the word *habitat* interchangeably with *neighborhood*. Increase the usage, gradually completely replacing *neighborhood* with *habitat*.

Take the children to a field. Define the boundaries. Children automatically run in a field; let them. If you want some control, you can suggest running games such as, "Can you run to that rock like the wind" or, "Can you hop to me like a rabbit?" Let the children explore the field, but make sure they realize the definite boundaries you have set.

Allow the children plenty of time to experience each activity fully. Have them look up and see the sky, look down and see the grasses. Have the children close their eyes and face the sun, feeling the warmth. Tell them to spread their arms wide to the sun. Make mental notes about the children's feelings as they play in the field. Children are usually excited, noisy, and happy in a field.

Place a preschool thermometer in the field. As the arrow rises, discuss this with the children: "It's very warm in the field."

Have the children each collect one thing to take back to the classroom. Place these in a large bag. If there is a live insect or spider, place it in a large jar covered with cheesecloth. Small children collect much better with their hands than with sweep nets.

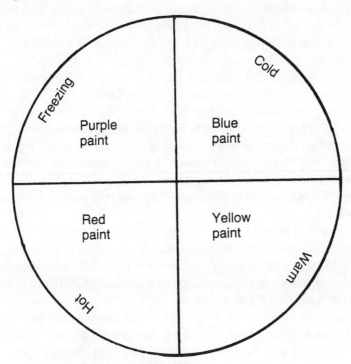

Preschool Thermometer

1. Obtain a round, outdoor thermometer.
2. Paint according to the chart above.
3. Label it Freezing; Cold; Warm; Hot.

Have the children lie down in a circle and ask them to close their eyes and listen. Walk around the inside of the circle, talking quietly, until they have settled down and can lie still. Say, "Listen." Tell them to raise their hands when they hear a sound. As the hands go up, talk about each sound and briefly mention whether or not it is a natural sound. Direct their attention, if necessary, to the field noises: the rustle of the grasses in the wind, the drone of the bees, the chirping of crickets, the cry of the hawk.

Indoors, after the children have settled down, ask them to relate their experiences in the field. As they talk, jot down their responses. From these conversations and from the mental notes you took in the field, write an experience story, illustrated with samples they brought in from the field. Watch the live creatures for the rest of the day, then release them back into the field.

Change the words to familiar songs to suit your experiences. I sing "Who Are the Creatures in Your Habitat?" to the tune of "The People in Your Neighborhood" using the grasshopper instead of the postman (see Resources).

Conduct a similar lesson in the forest. You'll notice that the children are quieter in the forest. Encourage them to walk softly. Have them pretend to be forest animals who move quietly. Have them listen to leaves moving in the wind. Listen to the bird songs. Note that it is darker than in the field.

Indoors, contrast the field and the forest. Include the children's actions and feelings as well as the animals, plants, temperature, and light intensity. Play the classification game, classifying animals according to whether they belong to the field or to the forest.

A note: A habitat can be smaller and more available than a field or a forest. You can study the sidewalk habitat that runs in front of your day-care center. Take its temperature. Discover what is growing, perhaps crawling, in the cracks. Compare and contrast this habitat with that of the sandbox habitat.

Field Animals

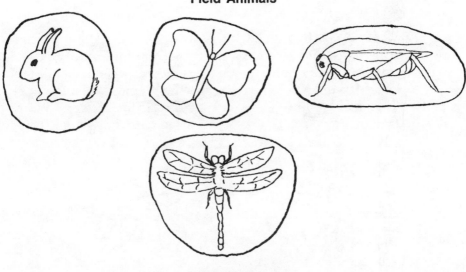

Forest Animals

Classification Game

1. Trace or photocopy the above animals.
2. Cut out circles and laminate.
3. Have children match rabbit, butterfly, grasshopper, and dragonfly to field.
4. Match sow bug, deer, woodpecker, and raccoon to forest.

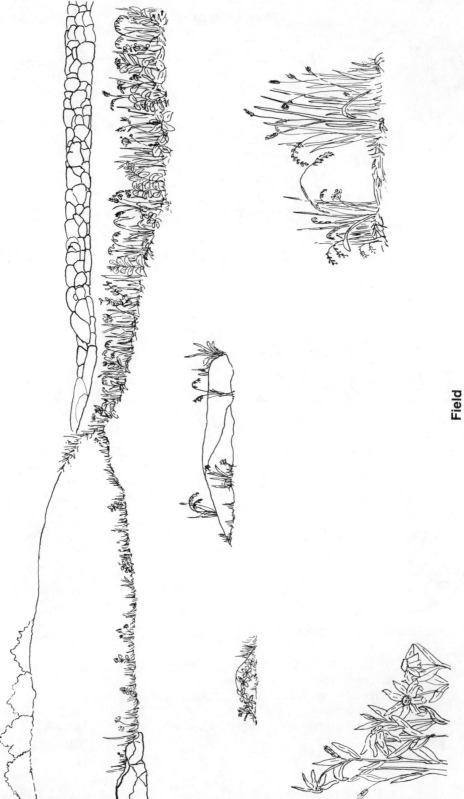

Field

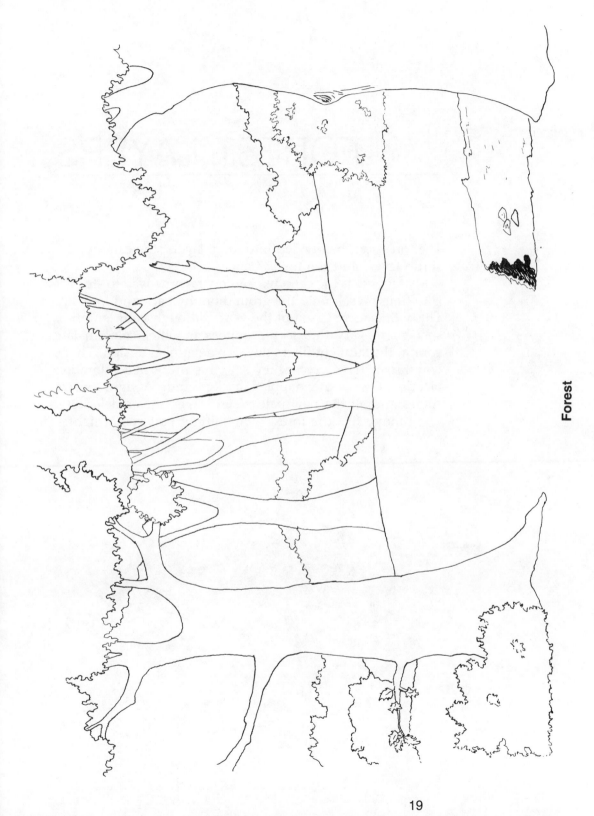

Forest

FOREST LAYERS

The forest can be divided into three layers: the canopy, the shrub layer, and the forest floor.

My favorite is the canopy. And my favorite way to study it is to fling myself onto the ground on my back and look up. This works any season of the year, although your length of stay might vary due to mosquitoes or bitter cold! In late spring, the sunlight filters down in a dappled design. That's why fawns have spots, they say; this protective coloration blends in with the dappled background. A light breeze comes and all the new pale green leaves shiver delicately. The canopy fills the forest with shifting patterns of light.

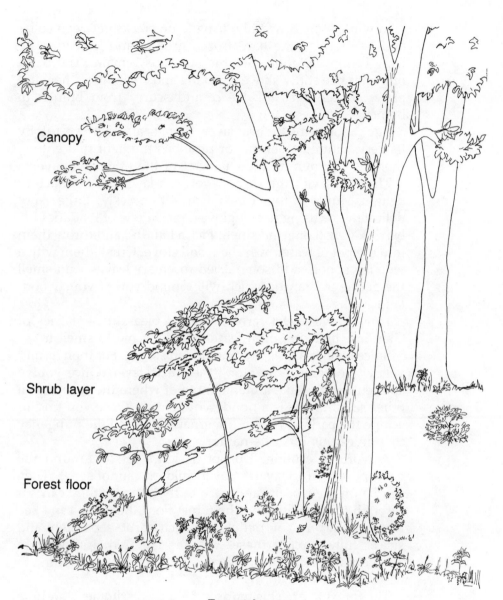

Canopy

Shrub layer

Forest floor

Forest Layers

In winter, dress warmly, leaving no cracks between collar and hat. Lay on the hard frozen ground and look up. The leafy canopy is gone, but the supports remain. The black branches rise stiffly above, cracking and creaking as the wind blows. Chickadees *dee-dee-dee* and scurry from branch to branch.

The canopy, the highest layer, is magical and powerful. By its very nature, it permits or prohibits the light that enters, thereby determining the character of the other two layers.

The next layer, the shrub layer, is a layer full of olfactory delights! Juniper: touch it—Ouch!—it's prickly. Either very delicately, or using heavy gloves, pick a few of its dark blue berries. Crush one and smell. Pick a handful and throw them into the pot of water over the wood stove. Crush them with a wooden spoon, add some dried rosemary leaves, and smell the gentle fragrance, which will remind you of your woodland walks.

How I love sweet fern! It evokes pleasant memories of Grandma breaking off a leaf and asking me to smell it.

Spice bush is a shrub to find first in spring. For then its airy yellow blossoms skim along the shrub layer. Once you've spotted them, make a mental note of where they are, for in other seasons this is a nondescript shrub. Once you find it, scrape the bark with your fingernail and smell the pungency that gives this bush its name.

A word of caution. Do not design a lesson around the concept of "shrub layer." Small children cannot see it. They can lie on their backs and gaze at the canopy; they can sift through the leaf litter on the forest floor. But they can't see the shrub layer. You *can* choose each shrub separately and successfully explore these with the children. Juniper is a good example. Children love to crawl under it, pretending to be rabbits in their forms.

The forest floor. This tends to be the preschooler's all-time favorite layer. All sorts of interesting creatures (salamanders, sow bugs) inhabit this dark, moist place. And preschoolers are the best ever at discovering them. They delight in sifting through the leaf litter, finding fungus, insects, and other tiny things that adults seldom spot.

UP, DOWN

Children, paradoxically, often learn what a thing is by learning what it is not. This is especially true with position words such as *up* and *down*. I mean, try to define *up*. I'll bet you can't do it—not without pointing your finger up and then shamefacedly muttering something about down.

So this is where we start. Point up. "This is UP." Point down. "This is DOWN." Use a high-pitched voice when saying *up* and a deep voice for *down*. Sing and act the "Up and Down Hokey Pokey" to the tune of the familiar version of "The Hokey Pokey."

> *You put your finger up, you put your finger
> down,
> You put your finger up and you shake it all
> around
> And then you do the hokey pokey and you turn
> yourself around
> And that's what it's all about!*
>
> *Verse 2: You put your arm up, you put your arm
> down . . .*
>
> *Verse 3: You put your head up, you put your
> head down . . .*
>
> *Verse 4: You put your leg up, you put your leg
> down . . .*
>
> *Verse 5: You put your whole self up, you put
> your whole self down . . .*
>
> *End by sitting down.*

Play the record and sing the "Sesame Street" song, "Up and Down." As you all sing it a second time, have the children place the items mentioned in the song (bird, airplane, ceiling, sky, sidewalk, foot, rug, ground) on a flannel board in the appropriate positions.

After the song, add more pictures of up-and-down items to the flannel board in proper locations, such as a helicopter, clouds, a flower, an ant.

Outdoors, gather into a circle and sing the "Up and Down" song again. This time, pause after singing, "I look up [point up] and see the [you supply]." Encourage the children to look up and add to the song. (Remember, their "up" is a lot lower than yours, so many of their responses which may seem "down" to you are in fact correct!) Sing again, "I look down [point down] and see the [you supply]."

Have the children lie down on the ground on their backs and look up. Encourage them to tell all they see that is up. When they mention tree leaves, supply the information that this is called a canopy. Use the word *canopy* in several short sentences and have them repeat it after you. For example, say, "The canopy of leaves is up above us. The canopy of leaves gives us shade." Then let the children complete the phrase, "The canopy of leaves. . . ."

Watch the activity in the canopy. Perhaps the wind shifts the leaves, or a squirrel scurries along, or a chickadee flits by. Once, in autumn, while with a group of boisterous, high-spirited two- and three-year-olds, I went into the forest. I managed to get them to lie in a circle and look up, but I didn't even try to get them to listen. It would have been futile. So they lay there, wiggling feet, waving arms, chattering excitedly. Suddenly a strong wind rose and shook loose scores of bright yellow leaves and down, down they floated. There was utter, complete, shocked silence. Finally, one child whispered, "Oh, look!" Gradually they all began to whisper, then giggle, then in pure joy, they ran to chase these golden gifts. That moment of wonder, the sudden, total, all-absorbing comprehension of leaves falling did more than any "circle time" discussion.

Listen to the canopy noises.

After the children get up, once more point up and say, "The canopy is above us." Then dramatically add, "And the forest floor is down."

Let the children explore a designated area of the forest floor. Time-honored naturalist methods such as "Here is a dead log, you and Tracy explore that," or the ol' circle-of-string method ("O.K., now, explore all within this string and don't go away from it") just don't work with young children—I know, I've tried them! Young children, like browsing goats, will go from spot to spot, sampling, until that one magic sow bug or salamander captures their total attention. Do, however, define broad boundaries. Preschoolers will spend forever sifting through leaf litter. They'll discover the tiniest buds, galls, fungus, and eggs you've ever seen.

Once indoors, substitute your up-and-down words to the tune of "Sesame Street's" "Up and Down." Use what your children saw, perhaps "canopy" and "chickadees," and "ground" and "ants."

RABBITS

One blue-skied day in early fall, I searched through a vacant city lot for a lesson idea. We had already done pigeons, starlings, dandelions, and ants. What I needed, I thought, was a good wild animal, and not a junkyard dog. It was 9:15 in the morning. About thirty feet away was the Head Start playground where scores of small children ran and screamed in the joy of being outside. The lot, situated on a busy street, was sandwiched between a business district and a residential area.

Suddenly, a rabbit darted in front of me! I couldn't believe it! In my notebook, I jotted down "Eastern cottontail," followed by several exclamation points. I began to wonder why the cottontail would choose this seemingly unlikely spot to live. I glanced across the street to the houses with their tiny lawns and even smaller vegetable gardens. Then I walked slowly through the knee-high weeds of the lot. Hmmmm.

Not such a bad place after all for Ms. Rabbit. Take-out food and protective shelter.

I walked on, amazed that I had actually seen a rabbit in the middle of the city, when suddenly a small mound of matted grasses caught my eye. I peeked through an opening and found a pair of shiny black eyes watching me intently. I had inadvertently discovered the rabbit's nest! The baby rabbit, or kitten, was as still as death. I rocked back on my heels and marveled. Overhead, planes were roaring, the traffic noise was constant, the children played loudly nearby. And amidst all this a wild animal was trying to survive—and evidentally was doing very well.

Nest of Eastern Cottontail

A baby rabbit is called a kitten.

Survival! The rabbit's entire existence is geared for survival. It has to be. For a rabbit has many predators including other animals, birds, and even people. Let's look at some of the physical adaptations that ensure its survival.

A rabbit's long ears can hear the approach of an enemy from any direction. Its nostrils move constantly to capture every scent. The large, appealing eyes are placed on the sides of its head, enabling it to get a good view in all directions. The long hind feet help the rabbit to run quickly or to jump great lengths away from its predators.

The old joke "breeding like rabbits" isn't one bit funny to our friend the cottontail. The female has several litters, producing as many as thirty young in a breeding season. Few survive to adulthood, as predators reduce this number drastically. The female gives birth in a nestlike depression made of grasses and lined with fur from her belly. This meager shelter gives little protection from either enemies or the wind and rain. The mother leaves the babies as often as possible so she will not betray their presence. Generally, she nurses them only at dawn and dusk.

Eastern Cottontail

At about two weeks of age, the young are out of the nest. The mother is now preparing for her new litter and can no longer afford to protect the older ones.

The Eastern cottontail's soft brown color is another protective device. It blends in perfectly with the dried grasses of vacant lots and fields. Although a rabbit can run fast, it can do so only for short distances. Its main defense is to remain motionless, melting into the landscape around it. It is said that even the rabbit's white tail helps it survive, that predators snap at this highly visible target and miss the whole rabbit.

VISUAL DISCRIMINATION

A person walking past that vacant lot full of dried weeds would never guess that not only did a rabbit live there, it was also raising its young in this small area. The idea of protective coloring intrigued me. What a fascinating way to develop visual discrimination skills.

First, acquaint the children with rabbits. If possible, find a domestic rabbit for use in the classroom. Call a local pet shop or the nearest 4-H Extension Center. Many people who raise rabbits are delighted to bring them into the classroom (see Resources for addresses of rabbit owners).

Allow children plenty of time to pet and observe the rabbit. Encourage their comments. You might discuss the following with the children: that the male is called a buck, the female a doe, and the baby, a kitten. Watch the rabbit's mouth and look at the long front teeth, which are needed for eating grasses and saplings. On the upper jaw are two sets of front teeth. Behind the long ones are short incisors. The long front teeth grow constantly, so the rabbit must always have something to gnaw on to keep them trimmed. Look at the rabbit's back feet and discuss how the animal moves by hopping and running. See the rabbit's long ears, which are used for acute, directional hearing.

The chances of a group of children spotting a rabbit in the wild are slim indeed. Walk to a likely rabbit habitat. Explain to the children that while the rabbit most probably will not be home, at least you can see where it lives. Discuss why a vacant lot would be a good home for a rabbit. Look for a rabbit's nest. If you are fortunate enough to find one, have the children feel it (if it's empty). Encourage the children to pretend to be rabbits. They can use their hands to make long ears. "Wiggle those ears. Now show me you can jump with those big feet." Allow enough time for the children to jump around. Review rabbit facts with the children: "A rabbit has long ears so it can easily hear its enemies. It has long hind feet to help it get away from those enemies. The long ears and the long hind feet help *protect* the animal from its enemies. The rabbit also does something else to protect it. It *hides*. It *sits very still*. I want each of you to find a spot to hide. I want you to sit there very still. Now I will try to find the rabbits."

As you walk around the field, you discover the "rabbits," finding the ones with the brightest clothes first. "Jason was easy to find because his red sweater is so easy to see. Janice is

Camouflage Rabbit

1. Trace this pattern onto different colors of construction paper, including brown.
2. Cut out enough rabbits so each child may find at least two.
3. Scatter in field.

easy to spot because she is wiggling. Oh, I had such a hard time finding Billy because he sat so still. And Laura is so hard to see because she is wearing brown pants. She blends in with the grasses."

While circling the field, feel free to become very dramatic. "I am a fox, a very *hungry* fox. And I am looking for nice sweet rabbits. AH! Here's one!" and gently hug the child you've discovered. Each child you find joins in a line behind you. After everyone has been found, walk the line of children into a circle and have them sit down. Note: children giggle and giggle. They love this simple game and want to play it over and over. Be sure to stop before their interest wanes, however.

Review who was easy to find and why (bright clothes and movement) and who was difficult to find and why (brown clothes that blended in and stillness). Feel free to use the term *camouflage*.

Have the children close their eyes and rest while you scatter construction-paper rabbits in the field. The children then try to find all the rabbits. When the red, orange, and purple rabbits are discovered first, discuss the reason with the children. The brown rabbits will take longer to find because they blend in. "Rabbits use their color to help hide, to help protect themselves. They blend in with the grasses so it is harder for their enemies to find them." Sometimes the children never do find all the brown rabbits. That's fine. Their camouflage is really working!

Indoors, give each child a rabbit cut out of an old grocery bag. They may glue on a cotton-ball tail. Then they can glue their rabbit onto a mural, onto a spot where the animal will be camouflaged.

At storytime, read *In a Meadow, Two Hares Hide* by Jennifer Bartoli (see Resources).

At snacktime, eat rabbit food: the children will enjoy preparing a simple salad.

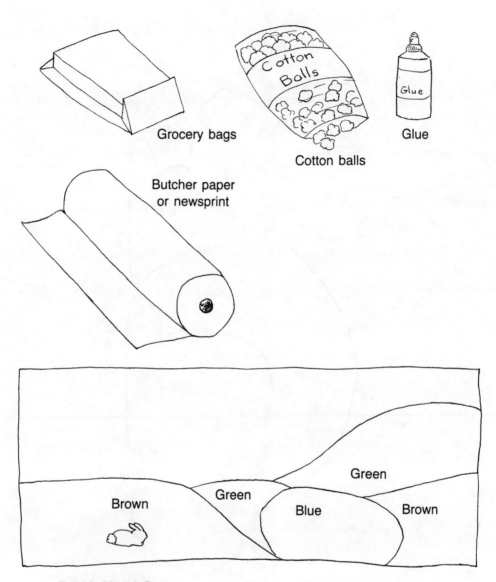

Grocery bags

Cotton balls

Glue

Butcher paper
or newsprint

Brown

Green

Green

Blue

Green

Brown

Rabbit Mural Game

1. Make rabbits with blackline master and grocery bags.
2. Have children glue cotton-balls on for tails.
3. With a long strip of butcher paper make a mural with areas
   of brown, green, and blue.
4. Children can glue their rabbits on a spot on the mural where
   the animal will be camouflaged.

Mural Rabbit

SEED DISPERSAL

Autumn is traditionally thought of as the harvest season. Squirrels scurry around storing acorns, while humans scurry around storing winter squash, freezing the last of the broccoli, and canning the tomatoes. But oddly enough, as we and our fellow animals are reaping, many plants are sowing. Sowing, and problem solving. O.K., you are a plant. It is fall. Daylight hours are growing shorter. It is time to make that last-ditch effort to secure your future. This is the problem. You are a milkweed; despised among men, you thrive in waste places in poor soil. The soil beneath your leaves will not support any more of your children—and you have produced hundreds of seeds. What do you do? A chill breeze blows, presaging winter. Shiver, and then—AHA!—you can send your seeds with the wind. Milkweed pods split open, releasing many seeds. Attached to each seed are strands of silky hair. Thus supplied with a parachute, off they fly in search of suitable ground in which to grow.

Then there is tenacious burdock. Honest to Pete, this is one stubborn plant. Just try to uproot it. That long taproot anchors it fully in the ground. But it's the burs that get you. Animals brush the plant, even lightly, and the burs cling obstinately until they are pulled out by frustrated teeth or fingers and flung disgustedly to the ground—where a new plant will emerge next spring.

Common plantain is another plant that must live by its wits. Described in Roger Tory Peterson's wildflower guide as a "low, dooryard weed," it is attacked by humans as spoiler of lawns and source of allergies. Children yank off the leaves and feel the vein strip (this leaf is excellent for leaf rubbings, by the way). When plantain seeds are ripe, the fruit opens

35

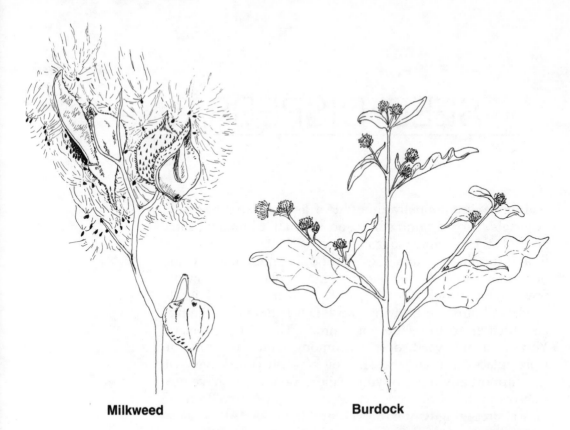

Milkweed   **Burdock**

around the middle. The seeds are small and light, easily
carried by the wind. Should the day be rainy, they give off a
sticky jelly. These jelly-covered seeds stick to any passerby,
to fall or be brushed off later, and then to grow.

PROBLEM SOLVING

As we have just discussed above, nature has posed a tricky
problem for some plants: how to plant their seeds at some
distance from the parent plant. This is especially tricky for an
organism that cannot walk, swim, or fly. And these plants
have met the challenge remarkably well.

Their ingenious solutions can provide interesting puzzles
for preschoolers. Give each child an animal you have cut
from colorful felt squares. Allow enough time for the chil-

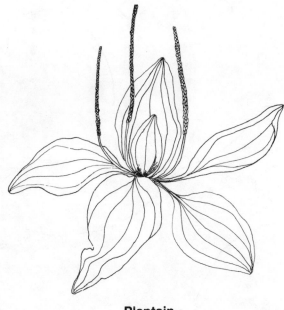

Plantain

dren to play with the animals, making their noises and movements.

Then, tell the children that it is time to take the animals for a walk. Outside, go past burdock, Queen Anne's lace, or other travelers. You go first, lightly holding your animal as it skims over these plants. Play follow the leader. Don't say a word.

You don't have to. Soon excited cries fill the air as the children discover the burs sticking to the animals.

With hand lens, examine the burs. Note how the tiny barbs hook into the cloth. Pull one apart and watch the seeds fall out. Mention to the children that these are traveling seeds, which have just hitched a ride on their felt animals.

Indoors, discuss how plants send their seeds to travel. Put some milkweed pods on a table. If you don't like huge messes, do this activity outside. Again, don't give any verbal directions other than to encourage the children to explore the pods. They will feel their shape and their texture. They will

Felt Animal Patterns for Seed Dispersal Activity

1. Purchase felt squares from a fabric store or discount store (about 25¢ each).
2. Use patterns to cut animal shapes from felt.

Optional: draw in features with fabric pen.

open one. Choose pods that are partially open, or the silks won't be fluffy enough to sail away. Examine the flat, brown seeds that are attached to the silk. See if the children can discover how these seeds travel.

Bring in some withered Queen Anne's lace (see Queen Anne's lace lesson on page 220 for a description of its "cups"). Let the children feel them. See if they can discover how these seeds travel. Make a collection of traveling seeds in your region. The following are examples: tickfoil, burdock, milkweed, dandelion, plantain, violet, jewelweed, cattails, thistle, maple wings, and goldenrod. Classify these seeds according to how they travel.

STARLINGS

Starlings in this country suffer from bad press. Not that it's undeserved, for these birds have surely become a nuisance. They have caused plane crashes. Their droppings accumulate several inches in cities. They nest early in cavities and holes, eliminating desirable nest sites for native birds. If they have ever come to your bird feeder, then you know how they devour food with no generosity to others. They take over. How could nature in its wisdom and balance allow this to happen?

Actually, the problem was created by humans. In 1890, a New Yorker, Eugene Schieffelin, imported 80 starlings from England and released them in Central Park. Imported species tend to do one of two things: Either they die fairly quickly due to unfamiliar habitat and food, or they adapt to the new environment and, having no native predators, thrive. Indeed, in time they can thrive so well, they usurp the native animals' food supplies and nesting sites. They, in short, become a royal pest.

Frankly, I had never paid much attention to starlings other than to give them an occasional disgusted glance. That is, until I paused one day long enough to watch them through preschoolers' eyes. A large maple tree grew in the city Head Start playyard. It was late September and we were gazing up at the red and gold leaves, when suddenly a dark, motley sort of bird landed on a branch. It disappeared into a hole in the trunk. A while later, out it came. The bird went in, the bird came out—and a nature lesson was hatched.

A close look at the starling reveals its rugged, tousled appearance. These birds molt in fall. The new feathers are tipped with white specks.

What were they doing, scouting for the nest cavity in fall? I wondered. Putting "dibs" on it until spring? No wonder our native birds are being shoved out; starlings have almost a half year's head start.

I began, grudgingly, to admire the starlings' survival ability. They do have their good points. Insect control, for one: A pair of starlings and their young consume tens of thousands of insects monthly. Like their fellow blackbird family members, starlings are smart. Because they are an imported species, they have had no natural migration patterns in the United States. But they soon learned that it is warmer in the cities. So by October, thousands of country cousins join the city starlings. They are also learning to migrate south from our native blackbirds.

As they fly in flocks, starlings are a joy to watch, swirling, shifting as one over the rooftops. They rival the Navy's Blue Angels for synchronized flying!

For a good read about a pet starling, read *Arnie, the Darling Starling* by Margaret S. Corbo and Diane M. Barras (see Resources).

Starling

INSIDE, OUTSIDE

Prepare for this lesson by making a starling puppet and a tree.

"This bird is a starling. It is sitting outside. Now the bird is going inside." (Put the bird in the hole.) "Where is the bird? Yes, it is inside the tree." Repeat this scene, giving each child the opportunity to follow your directions to either put the bird inside the tree or outside on the branch.

Go outdoors and watch the starlings swirl in the air, perch on the wires, feed on the ground. Perhaps you will discover a nest cavity, as I did. If so, observe the birds as they go in and out. When the bird goes inside the hole, whisper to the children, "The starling went inside its hole." And when it comes out, whisper, "The starling is outside."

Sing and act out "The Starling Song" to the tune of "Bluebird" (see Resources):

> *Starling, starling, in the hole,*
> *Starling, starling, in the hole,*
> *Starling, starling, in the hole,*
> *Oh, starling, you are resting.*
>
> *Starling, starling, out on the branch*
> *Starling, starling, out on the branch*
> *Starling, starling, out on the branch*
> *Oh, starling, you are playing.*

Watch as the flocks swirl overhead. Children may wish to careen around the playground in imitation of these aerial feats.

Provide a large, sturdy box and call it a hole in a tree. The children can "fly" in and out of it. If you are really ambitious, make a few starling costumes out of black cotton. Children can help by speckling them with white fabric paint.

Starlings are *noisy!* Record their sounds and listen to them indoors. Play musical chairs using the taped songs instead of music.

Pattern for Starling Puppet

1. Use a 2-pound oatmeal box to make the "tree."
2. Cover it with grocery bag paper and draw lines to resemble a tree trunk.
3. Cut a hole in the middle large enough for the Starling puppet; cut two small holes on the sides for a small branch to fit through.
4. The children can put the bird in the tree or out on the branch with a paper clip.

BLACK-CAPPED
CHICKADEE

Some of the best nature descriptions were written around the turn of the century. These writers not only studied nature, they lived with nature. Then too, life was more obviously dependent on nature. Hence, their writings are especially vivacious and involved with their subjects. The best places to find these gems are used bookstores. Also, watch your library's sale table.

One remarkable naturalist was Cordelia Stanwood. In 1905, at the age of forty, she began bird studies. On her property in Maine she observed, photographed, and wrote about birds. Initially denied employment because she was a woman, she eventually published articles and printed over five hundred bird photos.

Six Little Chickadees by Ada Graham (see Resources) is a delightful children's biography of Cordelia Stanwood. This book includes her photographs of six young chickadees whom she observed from the time their parents built a nest until they fledged.

Another woman who contributed to the field of environmental education was Anna B. Comstock. A woman of many talents, she developed a nature-study program for teachers. The final text, *Nature Study*, is still in print. The section on chickadees is a pleasant blend of information and the joy of chickadees. She writes of this bird who, amidst the rigors of winter, cheers us with its song, assuring us that "the world is all right and good enough for anyone." She describes a clutch of eight chickadee eggs that she discovered in an old fence post. She muses, "How these fubsy birdlings manage to pack themselves in such a small hole is a wonder; it probably gives them good discipline in bearing hardships cheerfully."

These cheerful birds delight preschoolers. Although they are small in size, chickadees are noisy and easy for preschoolers to see. Their markings make them easy for young children to identify, and their song says their name: *Chick-a-dee-dee-dee.*

Chickadee

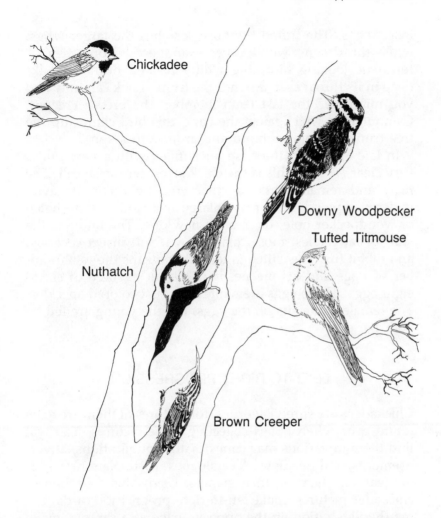

Chickadee

Downy Woodpecker

Tufted Titmouse

Nuthatch

Brown Creeper

This agile bird can be spotted dancing around the out-
ermost twigs of a tree or hanging upside down on a weed
stalk. It is searching for insect eggs and eats several hundred
of them in a day.

If you want to go bird watching, let the chickadee be your
guide. Follow it into the woods. Don't worry, you won't lose
this guide. It will flit and chatter overhead. Watch carefully
for a while, and you'll discover that they are part of a team.
No, not the A-Team, but this team is equally effective in
ridding the world of pests—in this case, insect pests. The
chickadees, of course, will be scouting the outer twigs for

insect eggs. The tufted titmouse searches the larger twigs, while the downy woodpecker examines the branches. A futuristic looking bird, the white-breasted nuthatch talks deep in its throat as it searches the trunk. Look carefully and you might see the last team member: the brown creeper. Camouflaged well against the bark, this bird climbs up the tree trunk by going around and around in a spiral.

In late February, the crisp air is filled with a new call, a very clear *Fee-Bee*. This is the chickadees' territorial call. The male and female work together creating the nest cavity in decayed wood. They may enlarge an abandoned nuthatch or woodpecker hole, or create a new one. The lining is the stuff of fairy tales: moss, plant down, soft insect cocoons, and rabbit fur. The clutch (a term that means the total number of eggs laid at one nesting) has an average of six to eight eggs. These eggs are white with rust-colored speckles. The female alone sits on the eggs, but the young are fed by both parents.

LEFT-TO-RIGHT PROGRESSION

Chickadees are surely favorites, for pictures of them are to be found everywhere. Start collecting these pictures. You will find them in various magazines, nature publications, advertisements, and needlework catalogues. Also, National Wildlife features them on their stamps. Using this collection of chickadee pictures, make left-to-right progression cards. Using the illustration on the opposite page as a sample, make your progression cards on poster board. Mine are six inches by twenty-four inches. Glue the chickadee pictures at either end of the poster board and draw wavy lines between them. Laminate them with clear plastic.

Have the children put their fingers on the chickadee to the far left and trace the flight pattern to the far right. (For naturalists with no early childhood training, this activity is an important reading readiness skill. In our culture, we read from left to right. This is a learned behavior.)

Make the large chickadee puzzle out of heavy oaktag or felt. The latter can be used on the flannel board. Separate the

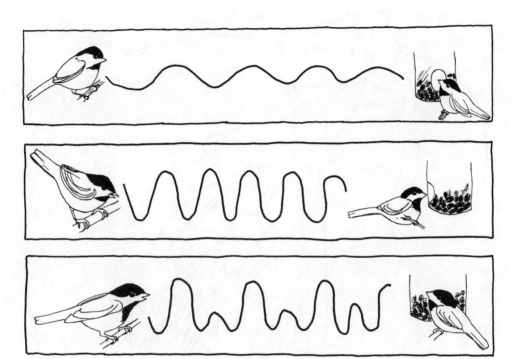

Left-to-Right Progression

body parts. Complete the puzzle except for the black cap and have the children put it in the right place, reinforcing their identification of this bird. Sing "Five Little Chickadees" (see Resources).

When you go outside, look for five chickadees. Count them. Perhaps you will be fortunate enough to find some nesting cavities. We found some in dead trees right on a well-used trail at a nature center. Note that chickadees are often found in the canopy. Lie on the forest floor, close your eyes, and listen for the chickadee calls.

Use a hand lens to examine twigs for insect eggs to discover just what that acrobatic chickadee is doing hanging upside down. Imitate the chickadee's movements: dance, do acrobatics, twirl. Indoors, read *Winter Tree Birds* by Lucy and John Hawkinson and *A Year of Birds* by Ashley Wolff (see Resources) to the children.

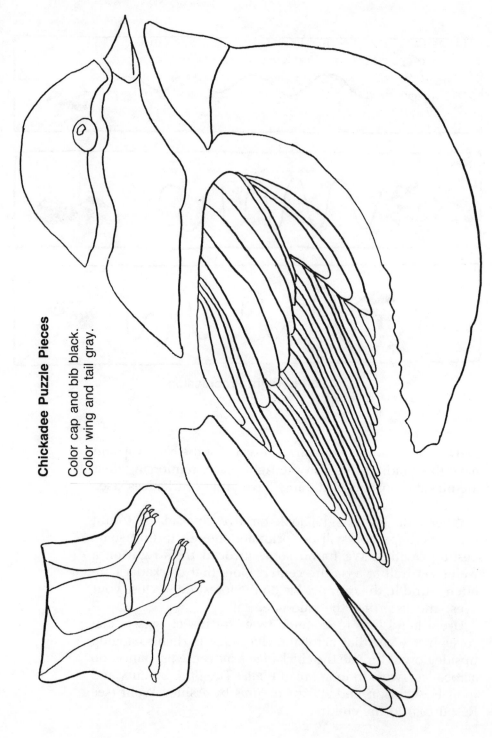

Chickadee Puzzle Pieces

Color cap and bib black.
Color wing and tail gray.

Using the chickadee puzzle, learn bird parts. Compare and contrast them to human body parts. Compare the activities of chickadees to those of the children. Make a large chart of these comparisons using magazine pictures. For example, one side can show pictures of birds preening, birds eating, and birds taking care of their young. On the other side, have pictures of children taking baths, children eating, and children with their parents.

STONE WALLS

My great-aunt died in February. On the day of the funeral, sleet fell from leaden skies. The mourners sat straight in straight-backed chairs around the gray casket. Stony eyes, unyielding Yankee faces. No tears here. Clipped phrases: "Twas better this way." "Past time for her to go." The minister, thin and hard in his eternal three-piece pewter gray suit, intoned the terse eulogy. I gasped for air in the rock-hard atmosphere, and glancing down, saw, with sudden shock, my gray wool skirt.

Many stories and jokes have been written about the old Yankee stereotype, who is described as having a dry wit and a hard, cold demeanor. There is a definite basis for these rumors. After all, anyone's character would be shaped by years—even generations—of wresting with rocks. Remember Peter Cabot's line in Eugene O'Neill's *Desire Under the Elms*? "Here—it's stones atop o' the ground—stones atop o' stones—makin' stone walls—year atop o' year."

It's true. You work all summer in the field and gardens pickin' stones. And this ain't nothing compared to what the early settlers did. Deep in our woods are miles and miles of stone walls: mute witness to their back-breaking chore. All winter we sit around the wood stove and bask in the warmth, congratulating ourselves on our cleared pastures. Then the snow melts in March to reveal—more rocks. Whoever classified rocks as inanimate objects did not live in New England.

Maxine Kumin, in her poem "Stones," speaks of these subterranean forces:

The moving of stones, that sly jockeying thrust,
takes place at night underground, shoulders first.

They bud in their bunkers like hydras. They puff
up head after head and allow them to drop off

on their own making quahogs, cow flops, eggs and
knee-caps. In this way one stone can infuse a colony.

Eyeless and unsurprised they behave in the
manner of stones: swallow turnips, heave graves

rise up openmouthed into walls and from time
to time imitate oysters or mushrooms.

The doors of my house are held open by stones and
to see the tame herd of them hump their backbones

as cumbrous as bears across the pasture in
an allday rain is to believe for an afternoon

of objects that waver and blur
in some dark obedient order.

As with anyone you struggle against for a long time, you develop a certain respect, even a grudging affection, for them.

The old-timers here in town speak longingly of the girls of their youth. Why, they had the shiniest, most lustrous hair. Do you know why? Well, it was their job to tend the sheep. Since the pastures were covered with rocks, grass grew sparingly between these stones. The girls would pick up the sheep by the hind end so they could nose in the grass amongst the rocks. They would then wipe their hair back with lanolin-oiled hands, creating those lustrous locks.

Rocks are part of the natural environment. People have used rocks to make walls—an artificial environment. Howev-

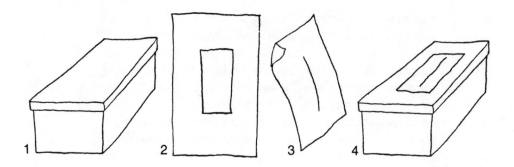

Feely Box

1. Shoe box
2. Cut hole in top of shoe box cover large enough for a student's hand.
3. Cut a piece of material the same size as the box cover, glue to the cover.
4. Cut a slit lengthwise in the material.

er, these walls have been naturalized over the years. Animals use them for homes. The many stone walls in New England are an important habitat for the chipmunk. These little animals use these walls as runways and as lookouts from which they can spot predators. The crevices in the rocks also provide them with shelter from predators. Other inhabitants are snakes, birds, and insects. Plants have been able to establish themselves on stone walls. Most frequently seen is lichen, a grayish green plant that is a combination of fungi and algae. Lichens are small, tough plants, and they do a gigantic task wedging themselves into cracks in the rocks. They secrete acids. Both these actions slowly cause rocks to crumble. Eventually the rocks are broken down into soil.

Stone walls are a sign of formerly cleared land. They were once boundaries for open pasture and croplands. Stone walls are a very definite heritage from the past. They, as much as old buildings and town records, should be preserved.

THE LETTER *G*

Late fall is a good time to explore stone walls. Foliage from the underbrush has died back enough so the walls are easy to find.

To begin your lesson, bring into the classroom a fist-sized granite rock. Place it inside the feely box. Blindfold one child at a time. Have the children feel inside the box and whisper to you what they think is in there. When all the children have had a chance to feel, open the lid and remove *the rock!* Say, "The name of this rock is granite. Can you say granite?" Pass the rock around and encourage discussion of its properties, including color, size, weight, and texture.

Tell them, "This rock is full of *g* words. This rock's name is granite. Its color is gray." If you want to extend the lesson, find granite rocks with lichen growing on them. Then you can add, "This gray granite rock has green lichen growing on it." Have the children repeat the *g* words. Leave the granite rock in an easily visible place and occasionally during the day refer to it. For example, ask them, "Is the granite still there?

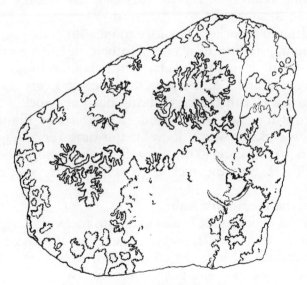

Granite with Lichen

Does it move? Does it eat? Does it make noises?" Allow ample opportunity for the children to get to know that rock.

Outdoors, take the children to a stone wall. Remind the children that they cannot walk on top of it but must walk alongside it. You'll need to repeat this reminder, but it is necessary because old stone walls contain loose rocks, which make footing treacherous for the preschooler.

Playing follow the leader, walk the length of the stone wall. Go slowly. As you go, encourage children to feel the rocks, the lichen, and the mosses. This is a terrific tactile lesson because the rocks are hard, perhaps cold, the mosses are so soft, the lichen so scratchy and rough. Smell the rocks. Look for holes in the wall where small animals might live. Look for signs of animal life on the wall. Often a large, flat stone will have empty hickory nuts or acorns on it providing a good lookout while Mr. Chipmunk or Squirrel eats his lunch.

Count the rocks in one section. Ask, "How did this wall get here?" Feel the temperature of the rocks. Check both sides of the wall. Are there differences in temperature, in plant growth, in shade or light? What is on top of the wall?

Indoors, read *What Did the Rock Say?* by George Maxim Ross (see Resources).

Children love rocks. They love to pick them up and bring them home, adding to a pile of rubble in their rooms, or hiding them deep in pockets, which later confounds the washing machine. Capitalize on this interest. Every time you go for a walk with the class, bring back one rock. Write a brief story for each one, include where it was found and what the children were doing at the time. Encourage the children to contribute to the story. Read these stories often to the children. Sort the rock collection by size, shape, and color.

Make the chipmunk wall.

After the children are inundated with rocks and are familiar with the term *granite*, and can use it verbally in conversation, introduce the letter *g* again. Have the children cut "g's" from old magazines and paste them onto a sheet of paper. Make or buy green finger paint.

Chipmunk Wall

1. Draw a stone wall on the back of a manila envelope, using this illustration as a guide.
2. Paint stones with gray paint.
3. Cut three slits as shown.
4. Mount three chipmunks on heavy paper.
5. Slip each into one slit.

Children may raise and lower the chipmunks as they wish.

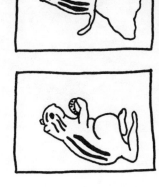
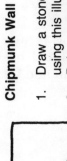

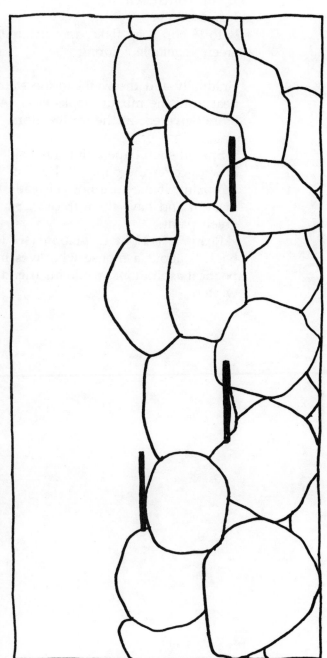

Green Finger Paint

½ cup cornstarch
1 quart water
¼ to ½ cup soap flakes (*not* detergent)
green vegetable coloring

Gradually add the water to the starch. Cook over medium heat until the mixture looks clear. Add coloring. Cool. Store, covered, in the refrigerator.

Spread shelf paper with shiny side up. Show the children how to cover the paper with paint. Have them make *g*'s in the paint. If they are not yet ready to make the letter, you make it and have them trace it. Say, "We're making *g*'s in green paint."

Read *Frederick* by Leo Lionni (see Resources). This picture book is about a mouse who lives in a stone wall and has poetical aspirations, while his friends toil in preparation for winter.

WINTER

Color
Recognition

Winter is an ideal season to teach colors to preschoolers. All other seasons have their colorful distractions: lush green of summer, flaming gold of autumn, hopeful yellow of spring. Only winter, with its unyielding scene of gray, provides a suitable background for learning colors. For when a color does appear against this drab landscape, it is startling in its intensity. Children must notice and pay attention. A male cardinal against the snow says to small children, "Look at me. I am red!" The preschooler has no choice but to attend to this bit of brilliance.

The lessons that follow develop and teach a colorful series of winter nature explorations for preschoolers. These explorations include readiness activities that enhance the concept of color. Decorate your classroom in the color of the day with crepe-paper streamers and magazine pictures. Wear that color. Send notes home to parents the day before for the children to bring in an object of that color or to wear something in that color.

CARDINALS

Field identification of the cardinal is easy for the preschooler. The male is our only red bird with a crest. In winter, his feathers are dusted with sooty gray. The flamboyance of the male heightens the elegance of the female. She is dressed in bronze with an edging of red.

Remember the old southern saw about the relatives who came to visit for three months and ended up staying for thirty years? Why, the food was so abundant, the hospitality so warm, that they just settled in! So it is with that crested redbird. Originally found only in our southern states, the cardinal has wended its way north. Are the winters warmer than before, the bird feeders more numerous, or the hedgerows and gardens of suburbia more inviting? Whatever the reason, the cardinal has settled in.

Once established in its territory, the cardinal is a homebody. It does not migrate in search of winter food. Rather, its omnivorous summer diet changes to that of just seeds, grains, and fruits. One of the prettiest sights in winter is that of a cardinal perched on a barberry bush eating the last of the dark red fruits. Children will enjoy attracting this bird to feeders by putting out sunflower seeds. As the cardinals feed, note their thick bills, which identify them as members of the grosbeak family.

Changing diet is one adaptation to winter's rigors. Feeding frequently is another. Surviving the cold is a full-time occupation. That classic pose of the fat cardinal on a snowy branch is in reality another survival tactic. For the bird is fluffing up its feathers to create more air pockets to insulate against the cold.

Cardinal

The gray tips of the male's feathers gradually wear off, leaving the scarlet breeding plumage. In late winter, the male starts to sing to the female and, unusual among birds, she answers. After choosing a mate, the female builds the nest of twigs, vines, leaves, and bark strips, and lines it with fine grasses. There are several reported cases of two female cardinals sharing the same nest—even of cardinals and different species of birds sharing the same nest. The incubation period for the brown-and-white mottled eggs is about twelve days. The babies are altricial, that is, born naked and helpless. They grow quickly, however, fledging at about ten days.

RED

Cardinals are the bright birds of winter. The lesson about them focuses on the color red. Children can engage in a variety of activities designed to teach recognition of the color red. Bird shapes can be cut out of many colors of construction paper. The children's task is to find the red ones. Christmas wrapping paper with a cardinal motif can be mounted on cardboard. Again, the children find the red birds and count them. Read the poem "What Is Red?" from *Hailstones and Halibut Bones* by Mary O'Neill (see Resources).

Make a cardinal puppet from red felt. He can appear and discuss his color with the children. He then directs attention to his large beak, which is ideally suited for cracking seeds. He passes out sunflower seeds, encouraging the children to feel how hard they are. Mr. Cardinal is also very proud of his crest. Mount several cardinal photographs, gleaned from *Ranger Rick* and *Your Big Backyard,* on construction paper and laminate them. The puppet can use these to continue discussion of his thick beak and the showy crest of the cardinal. Thus, children can easily learn some field identification and natural history.

Bundle up and go outside. The crisp cold air encourages the children to fly like cardinals and to hop in the snow looking for seeds on the ground. After learning two cardinal calls—*cheer, cheer* and the whistle that sounds like a person whistling for a dog—the air will be filled with preschooler cardinal songs and vigorous flapping.

Have the children form a large circle and play "Here Stands a Redbird." This is how this adaptation of a traditional American folk tune goes:

> *Here stands a redbird, tra-la-la-la*
> *Here stands a redbird, tra-la-la-la*
> *Sing, cardinal, sing.*

The teacher then points to a child who sings like a cardinal. Small children enjoy the repetition as they sing this song again and again. Each child gets a turn to whistle or "cheer."

Cardinal Puppet

1. Trace or photocopy pattern pieces.
2. Glue pieces as shown on pattern.
3. Sew back to front (A to A, B to B, etc.).
4. Sew head to back along D lines.
5. Open mouth, sew on mouthpiece along edge.
6. Sew on wings and crest.

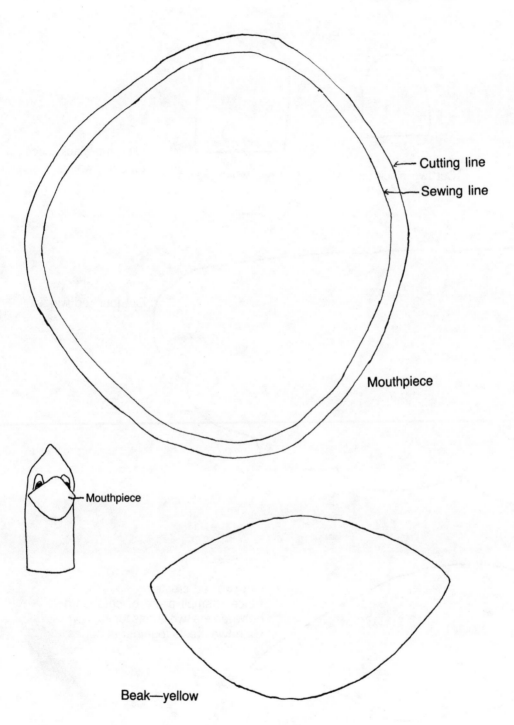

Cutting line

Sewing line

Mouthpiece

Mouthpiece

Beak—yellow

Eyes

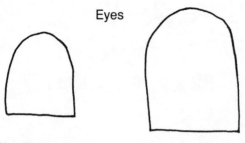

Cut two black pieces.   Cut two white pieces.

Glue the black piece onto the white.

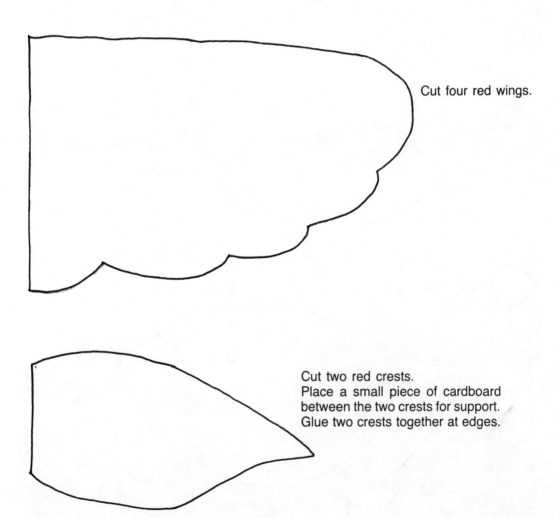

Cut four red wings.

Cut two red crests.
Place a small piece of cardboard between the two crests for support.
Glue two crests together at edges.

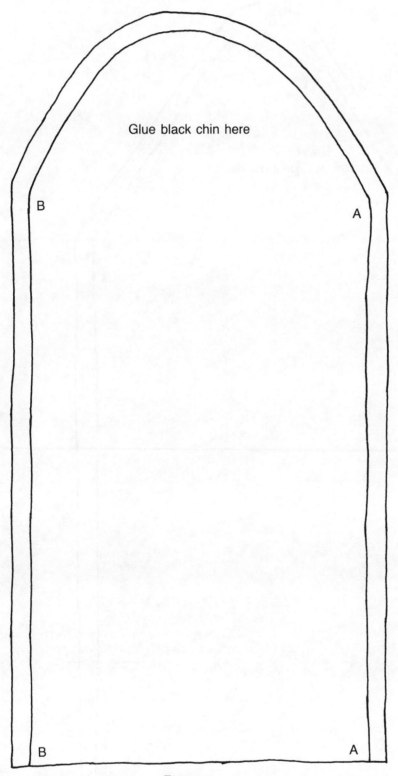

Glue black chin here

B   A

B   A

Front

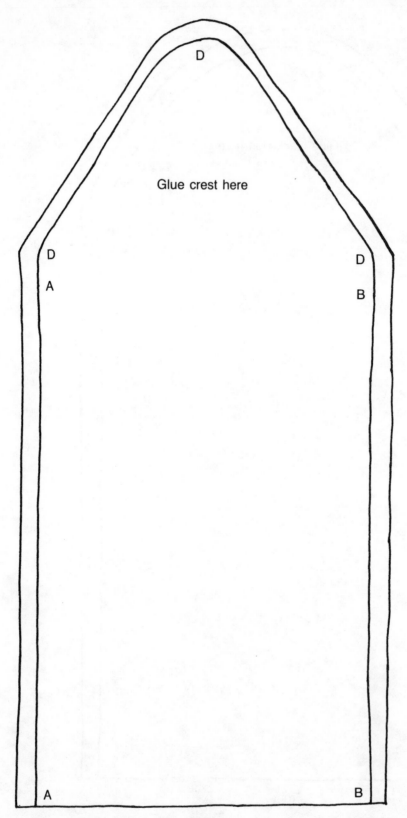

Glue crest here

D

D
A

D
B

A
B

Back

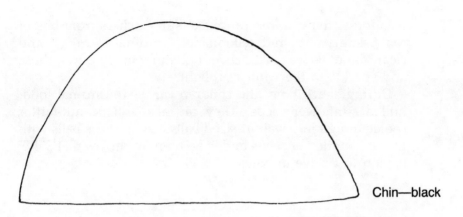

Chin—black

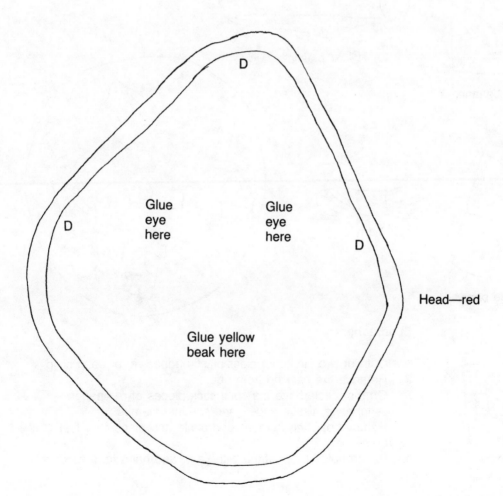

D

D

D

Glue
eye
here

Glue
eye
here

Glue yellow
beak here

Head—red

Construction paper

Indoors, the children can make sun catchers from bits of red tissue paper, red cellophane, "cardinal stamps," and clear self-adhesive plastic covering. Hung in windows, these add sparkle to the winter sunlight.

During snack time, the children can taste cardinal food: hulled sunflower seeds. They can also roll peanut-butter cookie dough into walnut-sized balls. Cover these balls with toasted sunflower seeds and bake them in the oven at 375°F for ten to twelve minutes.

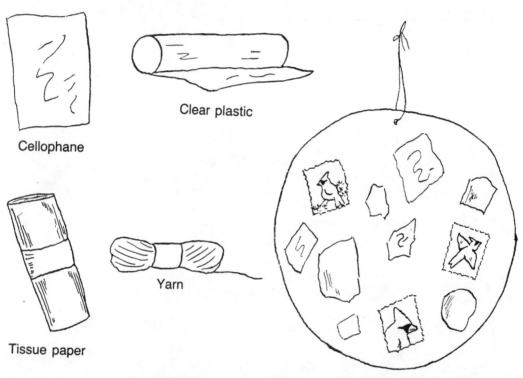

Cellophane

Clear plastic

Tissue paper

Yarn

Suncatchers

1. Cut out two circles of clear plastic adhesive for each child.
2. Remove the backing from one.
3. On that circle have the child stick pieces of red paper, cellophane, tissue paper, and cardinal stamps.
4. Remove backing from second circle and place over first circle.
5. Punch hole in top, string with yarn, and hang from window.

Stamps

SNOW

During a power failure one winter when water supplies dwindled, we scooped up buckets of snow and set them near the hearth to melt. The children learned three important lessons:

1. The snow turned into water.
2. There were dust particles floating on the surface of the melted snow.
3. It sure takes an awful lot of snow to make a little bit of water.

What is snow? Yes, snow is made up of droplets of frozen water vapor. These droplets have formed around a tiny speck of dust or some other material. Snow crystals grow into many different forms, but all are hexagonal. At the turn of the century, W. A. Bentley photographed hundreds of crystals. His 1931 publication, *Snow Crystals,* is now available as a reprint (see Resources). Small children and adults both enjoy poring over these pages.

Snowstorms definitely affect human activity, causing snarled traffic, closed schools, and impassable driveways. The natural world is also affected by snow. A thick layer of snow protects the ground from alternate periods of freezing and thawing. The amount of snow also influences the activities of winter animals. A small snowfall benefits the animal world by hiding small animal runs from predators. Deep snow makes it easier for rabbits to reach high branches to nibble. Snow, with its insulating air pockets, provides warmth for the grouse who dives into it. On the other hand, animals must expend more energy getting through the snow searching for food.

WHITE

The sky is low, the clouds are mean,
A travelling flake of snow

Across a barn or through a rut
Debates if it will go.

A narrow wind complains all day
How someone treated him:

Nature, like us, is sometimes caught
Without her diadem.*

Emily Dickinson is so right. That late November day that delivers the first snow is most unpleasant. There are times when nature wants to be alone, and this is one of them. Make only a brief trip outdoors with the children. Children reflect the weather; they, too, will tend to complain. So, quickly! Ask them to look up at the sky and watch the snowflakes float down. Tell them to hold out their arms to catch the drifting flakes on their sleeves. Catch a few flakes on a piece of cardboard, which has either been painted black or is covered with dark fabric. Use hand lenses to examine these snowflakes. On this uneasy day, the children's attention will evaporate as quickly as the snow does. It is raw. It is time to go in—to security, to warmth.

Indoors, the children will be restless and on edge. Soothe them with warm mulled cider, cheese, and crackers. Read them a brief story, such as *Sky Dragon* by Ron Wegen (see Resources).

Have the children lie on the floor and close their eyes while you say in a slow, droning voice:

You are the ground
You make no sound
You feel so old
You are so cold

*Dickinson, Emily. "The sky is low, the clouds are mean." *American Poetry and Prose.* Norman Foerster, ed. Houghton Mifflin, 1957. Used with permission of the publisher.

You are waiting
Shhhhhhhhh
Waiting for snow.

The snow comes down
The snow lands on the ground
The snow is so deep
The snow puts you to sleep.
Shhhhhhhhhhh
Shhhhhhhhhhh.

At this point let them lie quietly, if they will, or perhaps listen to George Winston's piano solo, "Snow" (see Resources). Later, the children can play with the Snowflake Game. Today is not the day to learn about the natural history of snow. It is a day of survival. Have no expectations. Just be there.

For a while, there is no more snow. The cold seeps in. The landscape stiffens. Then one morning you wake up before the alarm goes off. Something is different. It is utterly quiet. You feel content and cozy. Outdoors the world has changed: "We looked upon the world unknown. . . . The old familiar sights of ours Took Marvellous shapes." as John Greenleaf Whittier wrote in "Snowbound." The entire world is white. And what a white! It sparkles and glistens and invites. Children need no second invitation. Out they race to run, jump, and slide.

When the first exuberance has subsided, call the children together into a circle. Walk around the inside of this circle and draw attention to your tracks. Note that there are two footprints to every complete set of tracks. Note that the tracks are close together. Note the pattern of walking. Now run around the circle and note the difference. The tracks are further apart. Play follow-the-leader, having each child step as precisely as possible into the preceding tracks. Vary the steps: walk, take long strides, tiptoe, run, hop.

Snowflake Game

1.   Photocopy or trace the snowflakes.
2.   Glue onto cardboard.
3.   Cut each snowflake in half; laminate each half.
4.   Mix up the halves and have the children find the matching halves.

Indoors, read "What Is White" from *Hailstones and Halibut Bones* (see Resources). Enjoy a white snack of popcorn, cottage cheese, or milk. Sing "What Color Is the Snow on the Ground":

> *What color is the snow on the ground?*
> *What color is the snow on the ground?*
> *WHITE!*
> *White snow, bright snow, sunlight, bright white*
> *snow!*

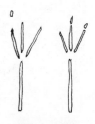

Bird Print

Draw footprints on a length of brown paper and have children match their strides to these.

Introduce the tracks of familiar animals: a cat, a dog, and a bird. If possible, bring in a gentle, child-loving dog and examine its feet. Note the pads and the claws, as well as the number of feet. Match the tracks of these common animals to pictures of these animals.

Outdoors, follow some dog or cat tracks. Children love to see where the tracks go. Find some bird tracks and discover that they end abruptly. Where did the bird go, and how?

Cat Print

Small children who come to nature centers and walk the trails expect to see animals. And, of course, any self-respecting diurnal animal will scoot the second it hears preschool chatter. That is why tracking is such a treat for preschoolers. At last there is concrete evidence that wild animals really do live here!

The naturalist Edwin Way Teale wrote in *Wandering Through Winter* (see Resources), "Snow is the great revealer. It cannot keep a secret. All through the woods around us it was filled with the gossip of the night." Children delight in discovering tracks: "Oh, here are some and here are some *more*." In their enthusiasm they tend to obliterate the tracks, so show them how to stand to one side beside the tracks, not on them. Don't be alarmed when they completely forget your careful instructions as they stomp on the next set in the great excitement of discovery.

Dog Print

Walk Pattern   **Run Pattern**

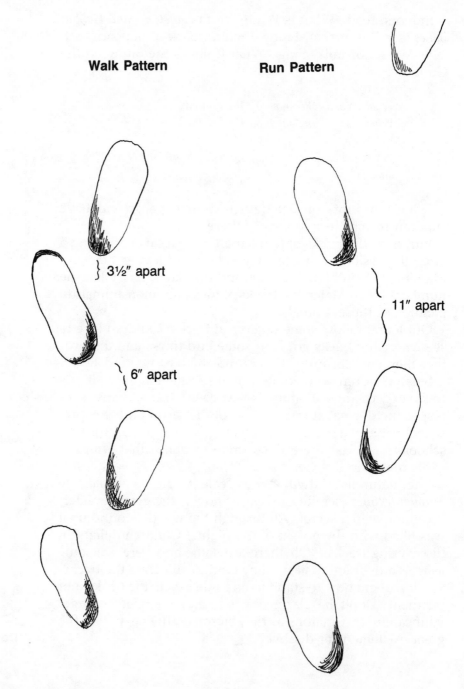

3½" apart

6" apart

11" apart

Tiptoe Pattern   **Jump Pattern**

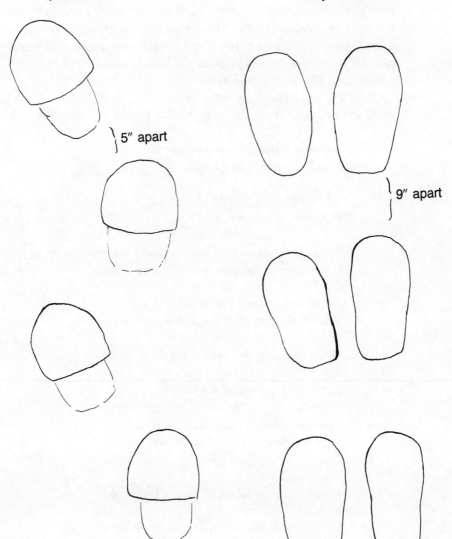

5" apart

9" apart

Some children will want to follow the tracks, to guess what the animals' activities were. Other children are only interested in finding tracks. Discuss identification only when you have a very clear print. Snow conditions, ice, and wind can all alter the tracks, making identification difficult and frustrating for small children.

Indoors, read the following poem, "Animal Tracks," and match the tracks of each verse to the picture of the animal.

Snow is falling; birds have gone away
It is bare and it is gray.

Snow is falling; birds are calling
Come away; come away.

Snow has fallen; bird must come back
It hops near the tree and it leaves a track.

All of a sudden I see another track
With little feet in front and big ones in back.

Walk through the snow and soon you will
spy
Little bitty prints of a mouse running by.

See the chewed bark high on a tree
A porcupine has been there. He's eaten for
free.

It's time to go home. I take a last look
around
O see the flash of white, a deer is off with a
bound.

Snow has fallen; it's a very good time
To take a walk in the woods to see the
animals' signs.

Mouse Tracks	**Bird Tracks**	**Rabbit Tracks**

Porcupine Tracks   **Deer Tracks**

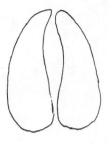
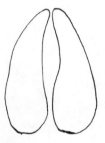
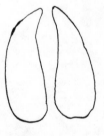

84

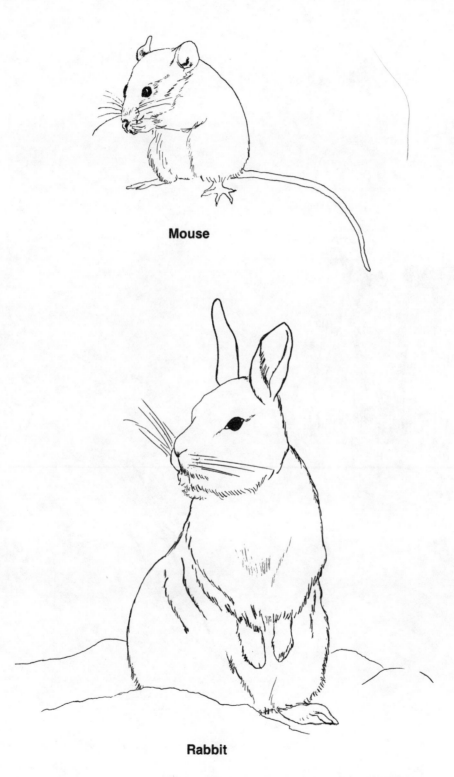

Mouse

Rabbit

85

Deer

Bird

You can make plaster-of-Paris tracks easily with the children. First, mix the plaster of Paris with enough water to make a mixture with the consistency of heavy cream. Pour it into small aluminum-foil loaf pans (they should measure about 6 inches by 3¼ inches by 2 inches). You do not have to oil the pans. Let the mixture thicken until it is the consistency of modeling clay. Now, press replicas of animal feet into the plaster, then remove them. You can either order replicas from Museum Products (see Resources) or make your own out of heavy cardboard. If you make your own, cover the cardboard with clear adhesive paper so the plaster won't stick to them. Allow prints to harden. They can then be removed easily from the pans and used as paperweights or decorations. Children can also paint them.

Porcupine

Inside the 🏠 you're snug and warm.
Sheltered from the winter ❄️.
Look out the 🪟 at the ❄️.
It calls to you. It says "Let's go!"
But wait! You can't go out like that!
You must put on 🧥 👢 👢 🧤 🧤 🎩
Now you're outside, look around.
There's ❄️ ❄️ everywhere. It covers the ___
Take off one 🧤 and feel that ❄️ ❄️,
Throw it up high and throw it down low.
Rub some ❄️ ❄️ on the side of your 😊.
Then put on your 🧤 and run a race.
Stop! Don't move! Just quietly stand.
Be very, very still. Listen to the land.
Close your 👁️ 👁️, and stand up straight.
What? You're feeling colder? You don't want to wait?
O.K. To get warm just run around.
Run through the ❄️ ❄️ and then fall down.
BRRR! I'm cold! How about you?
Let's go inside for a warm drink or two.
Later when your nap is done,
We'll come back outside and have more fun!

WOODCHUCK

Last summer, a woodchuck visited my vegetable garden and nibbled the tender young bean leaves. Ah well, I said philosophically, at least I planted generously in the old tradition so there is enough for all. Well, either ol' Woodchuck isn't much of a philosopher or he hadn't heard of that tradition. For on subsequent trips he demolished all the beans, not to mention the broccoli, the peas, the. . . . We marshalled our forces and put up a fence. And watched as the varmint burrowed under it. Then we invested in an electric fence charger (the vegetables are now pretty expensive). After days of clipping weeds around the garden's perimeter, stringing wire, putting up insulators and plastic fence posts, the work was done. Two days later, after all this effort and expense, our dog caught the woodchuck. We, as Maxine Kumin writes, lapsed pacifists, praised the dog and photographed his catch.

Woodchucks, or ground hogs as they are called in some regions, evoke definite responses. Its one day of glory is on February 2, Ground Hog Day. With cameras from the "Today" show aimed at his burrow, poor Punxsutawney Phil is roused from his burrow to prophesize the length of the remainder of winter. If a ground hog sees its shadow on February 2, so the story goes, there will be six more weeks of winter. If it doesn't, spring is right around the corner! Ironically, all other woodchucks miss all this, for they are hibernators who do not awaken until much later. Ground Hog Day is the American version of a European holiday. February 2 is Candlemas, a religious festival honoring the time when Mary brought the infant Jesus to the temple. It is a day when candles to be used in the coming year are blessed. The English and Germans watch for the shadow of a hedgehog or a badger, which are not hibernators, to predict spring's arrival.

Oh well. It's fun. Besides, by February 2 we need some nonsense!

Why is the woodchuck a hibernator? He is strictly a vegetarian. Obviously, green plants are few and far between in the dead of winter, so this creature has adapted to winter's rigors by sleeping right through it. Not a bad idea.

The woodchuck prepares for this sleep by eating its way through summer until it is quite fat. Around the first of October, it snuggles into its grass-lined room within its burrow and sleeps until the end of February or the first of March.

A full-grown woodchuck is about two feet in length (although I swear the one in my garden was the size of a sheep). The brownish fur is coarse and thick. The skin is tough and loose. As it walks, it seems to "pour along," as Anna Comstock wrote. Both pairs of feet have long claws, which are used in digging holes and burrows. These burrows are ingenious affairs. The front door is surrounded by piles of dirt, and no attempt is made to camouflage it. This entrance opens to a long, slanty tunnel, which eventually straightens out. Along this tunnel are rooms for nesting, and, at the end, a grass-lined room for sleeping.

Other entrances are concealed for safety. They may be surrounded by tall grasses, for example. There is no dirt around these holes. The woodchuck has scooped it all the way to the front door.

Woodchucks mate early after awakening in spring. After one month's gestation, the young are born. By midsummer, these young are independent enough to move out, establishing their own territories. Woodchucks do not use the same burrow year after year. Their abandoned holes provide shelter and escape for other mammals.

Just as a postscript, I'd like to add that while thumbing through *Joy of Cooking*, I found a recipe for woodchuck. Hmmmm. Maybe next year. . . .

Woodchuck

BLACK

Now a media event, February 2 is a good time to learn about hibernation. Today, as you discuss seasons, linger on winter, stressing the adaptations required for winter survival. Children, for example, wear heavy coats; they don't play outside as much as they did in summer; and they drink hot soup to keep warm. Some animals simply cannot find food because most green plants have died. And so these animals, including the woodchuck, sleep all winter. They awaken slowly in spring when their food supply is growing again.

Read the following poem to the children.

> Once upon a time, way back last summer,
> Once upon a time, when the leaves were
> green,
> Once upon a time, there was a furry, fat, fine
> woodchuck.
>
> Oh, woodchuck was furry—its coat was thick
> and brown;
> Oh, woodchuck was fat—it ate and ate all
> day long;
> Oh, woodchuck was fine—it was big and
> plump.
>
> Woodchuck's large front teeth bit off plants;
> Woodchuck's grinding teeth chewed them up.
>
> Woodchuck's sharp claws in front dug the
> ground;
> Woodchuck's sharp claws in back pushed out
> the dirt.
>
> Oh yes, woodchuck was busy—eating lots of
> plants;
> Oh yes, woodchuck was busy—digging a
> burrow;
> Oh yes, woodchuck was busy—eating and
> digging all summer long.

Eating and digging all summer long,
Eating and digging all summer long,
Eating and digging all summer long.

Then the seasons change and the days are
cooler;
Then the seasons change and the green
plants die;
Then the seasons change and the woodchuck
goes to bed.

Cold winter days—the snow falls softly;
Cold winter days—there's no food around;
Cold winter days—woodchuck sleeps and
sleeps and sleeps.

Again the seasons change; this time the days
are warmer,
Again the seasons change; this time the green
plants grow,
Again the seasons change; this time the
woodchuck wakes up!

Woodchuck stretches, yawns, and opens both
eyes;
Woodchuck stretches, yawns, and looks
around;
Woodchuck stretches, yawns, and finds a
surprise.

Now what do you think surprises the woodchuck?
Now why do you think it blinks its eyes?
Now what do you think woodchuck sees in
the sunshine?

Can you guess???!!!

Why woodchuck sees . . . woodchuck's
SHADOW!

Woodchuck

Woodchuck and Its Shadow

94

Read the story again, this time encouraging the children to dramatize the action.

Take a field walk to a known woodchuck hole or to a likely woodchuck habitat. While there, have the children act out the woodchuck cycle of summer feeding, winter hibernating, and spring awakening.

While outside, find shadows: the children's shadows, shadows made by buildings, plants, cars, a stray dog. Play shadow tag.

Once indoors, use the woodchuck box with the children.

Bring in natural items, such as twigs, stones, and leaves, and make shadows with them. Color these shadows with wide crayons or felt-tipped markers. For children who can't trace the shadow, outline it for them and then let them fill it in.

Read "My Shadow" by Robert Louis Stevenson (see Resources).

Woodchuck Box

1. Use a cardboard box approximately 13″ × 9″ × 9″.
2. Cover with brown paper (grocery bag) and cut slit in top.
3. Use a bright light source so woodchuck casts a good shadow.

Pattern for Woodchuck Puppet

Make from heavy cardboard.
Place in woodchuck box.

EVERGREEN

Winter is the time to learn nature's secrets. We have already discovered some of them as we tracked animals in the snow. But there are even more steadfastly held confidences.

One keeper of secrets is princess pine *(Lycopodium obscurum)*. Running quietly over the forest floor, she keeps her own counsel. Her erect posture is the remnant of a royal past and the silent acknowledgment of her present uniqueness. Princess pine is a member of the club moss family, an ancient lineage. Three hundred million years ago, in the Paleozoic era, club mosses grew to enormous sizes—one hundred feet tall and three feet in diameter. Just imagine these vast forest jungles, all green as there were as yet no flowering plants.

Go into the woods and look carefully. There, growing about six inches from the ground, is princess pine. Her present size gives no indication of her past glories. But admire her ability to adapt; her ability to accept less has ensured her survival.

This low-growing habit of club mosses helps them escape the drying effect of winter winds. They hug the ground and take advantage of the insulating snow blanket.

Feel the leaves of the teaberry or of the spotted pipsissewa. Notice how smooth and waxy these leaves are. This waxy coating helps prevent evaporation of life-sustaining moisture. Touch pine needles—how long and slim and pointed they are. What better shape exists to shed the snow?

Find rosettes of leaves. These rings of leaves stay green all winter, alive and warm close to the ground, under the protective snow.

Other evergreen plants to look for are the following:

Princess Pine

97

Teaberry

Spotted Pipsissewa

Christmas fern; juniper; cedar; white pine; spruce; spotted pipsissewa; rattlesnake plantain; mosses; rhododendrons, and mountain laurel.

GREEN

The two-year-old walking beside me looked up at the azure sky and exclaimed, "Oh, the sky is so green today!"

And then there was the time I led a kindergarten red-and-green walk. While all the children admired the flaming sumac and the verdant mosses, most were unable to say which was green and which was red.

This is definitely one time when color readiness activities are crucial to the nature lesson. Green is responsible for much preschooler confusion. Problems range from identification of the color to remembering the word *green*. Before you tromp through the woods or schoolyard in search of green, make sure your students know what green is!

The most effective, and fun, way to learn green is to become immersed in it. Wear green, drape the walls with green fabric, cover the windows with green cellophane. Then *make* green. Children seem to understand green better if it is made before their eyes, or, better yet, if they make green themselves.

Set out a piece of finger-painting paper (shelf paper, shiny side up, will do) in front of each child. In one corner of the paper, put a blob of blue finger paint; in another, a blob of yellow finger paint. Then, sit back and watch the children paint. First, they tippy-finger through the paint, then tentatively swirl with three fingers, and finally, throwing caution to the winds, cover their hands with paint—creating swirls, dots, and waves. Suddenly one child exclaims, "Look!" in amazement as green appears. "Green," you say happily, "You've made GREEN!"

Another way to create green is to put a few drops of blue food coloring into a baby-food jar filled with water. Watch as the blue slowly spirals down. Then add yellow. Cap the jar, then shake it. Presto! Green! Place the jar in a sunny window and watch the green shine through.

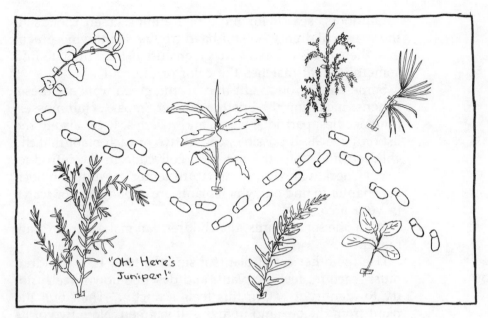

"Oh! Here's Juniper!"

Green Walk Mural

1. Stretch a large piece of butcher paper across the floor.
2. Tape plants along the paper.
3. Make a potato print in a foot shape, dip in green paint.
4. Have the children "walk" it across the paper.
5. Encourage the children to comment on each plant and write these comments on the paper.

Most children are already familiar with the "Sesame Street" character Kermit the frog. Purchase a Kermit puppet from a toy store or make one. To make your own, cut out a picture of Kermit from *Sesame Street* magazine, mount it on cardboard, laminate it, and attach a stick for a handle. Now the children can meet old friend Kermit and listen as he sings "Bein' Green." He can also read "What Is Green" from *Hailstones and Halibut Bones* (see Resources). Kermit can then introduce a royal friend of his, Princess Pine. She has brought two friends along, Creeping Jenny and Mountain Laurel.

Outdoors, search for more of Kermit's green friends. If there are children who still have trouble identifying green, give them cards colored with green and instruct them to find something that matches the color of the card.

Some plants you might find on the green walk are these: lichens, including the bristly reindeer "moss"; club mosses; pine needles; partridge berry, and rosettes. Refer also to the list on page 98. If possible, collect two of each plant that the children find. (See the notes on collection in the introduction.) Check with your local nature center or Audubon Society chapter to find out which plants are endangered or scarce in your area.

With one set of plants, the children can make a green walk mural.

Use the other set of plants inside the feely box. Children must reach in, feel the plant, and describe how it feels (not try to identify it): "Oh, this feels scratchy." Then pull the plant from the box and note that it is green. Note two of its properties: "This reindeer moss is green *and* it is scratchy." The plants may then be classified according to similarity (they are all green) or according to their textural differences.

INSECTS

Have you ever noticed how the young child is far more interested in an ant scurrying across the floor than in the marvelous lesson you just presented? By joining in that child's interest, you, too, will discover the fascinating insect world.

All insects have six legs; a spider with its eight legs is not an insect. Insects also have three body parts: the head, the thorax, and the abdomen. Insects also go through very drastic physical changes in their lifetimes. These changes are referred to as *metamorphosis.*

One type of metamorphosis is called complete metamorphosis, meaning transformation. And indeed it is quite a transformation. First the egg is laid. From this egg hatches the larva. The larva eats and grows. Eventually it forms a coating around itself and enters the pupal stage. People consider this the "resting" stage, as to the human eye there

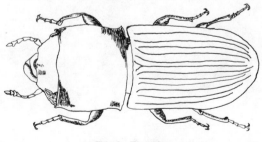

Bark Beetle

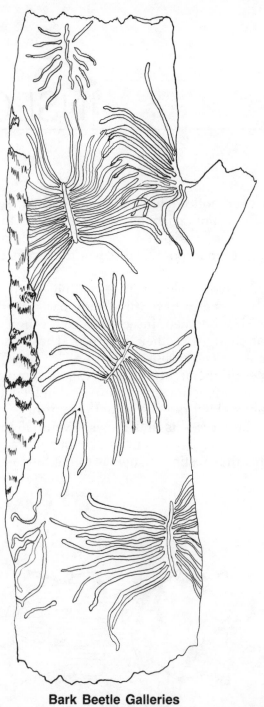

Bark Beetle Galleries

appears to be very little change from the outside. But inside, miraculous changes are taking place as the pupa becomes an adult.

Where are the insects in winter? All insects are cold-blooded, which means their temperature is equivalent to that of their surroundings. Insects rest in order to survive the winter. Each species has chosen one part of its life cycle in which to spend the winter. Mourning cloak butterflies, for example, overwinter as adults. So do ladybugs. These insects hide in crevices in bark and basically hibernate until spring. Ants hibernate underground.

You probably won't ever see a bark beetle. It spends most of its time in its burrow in the bark of a tree. The females excavate brood galleries and then lay eggs along the sides of them. When the larvae hatch, they eat the wood, making peculiar wood engravings. Once again the perpetrator in nature eludes us, but the tracks remain. To find these engravings, search for a fallen log and pull off the bark.

While you won't find many active insects in winter, you will find their abandoned homes or their egg cases. You have undoubtedly noticed galls before—those swellings on the dried weeds in the vacant lot, or those puffballs lying under oak trees. A gall is a swelling in a leaf, stem, or twig. These swellings are caused both by adult insects and by larvae, which irritate plant tissues and cause further swelling. Thus, larvae are at once protected within a snug, round home and supplied with food. There are hundreds of gall-producing insects, including species of wasps and flies.

Galls continue to be useful even after the original occupants move out (or are eaten). These homes shelter other insects in winter. These insects, in turn, are often eaten by hungry birds and mammals.

The praying mantis's egg case is one of those things you look for vainly year after year, never finding it. Then you finally spot your first one, and now you see them everywhere! You find them on grass stems, on wooden fences, even on the south sill of the house. These egg cases are about an inch long. Inside are scores of baby mantids, which will emerge in the spring.

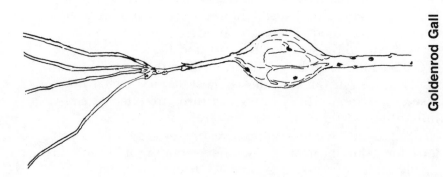

Cedar Gall

Goldenrod Gall

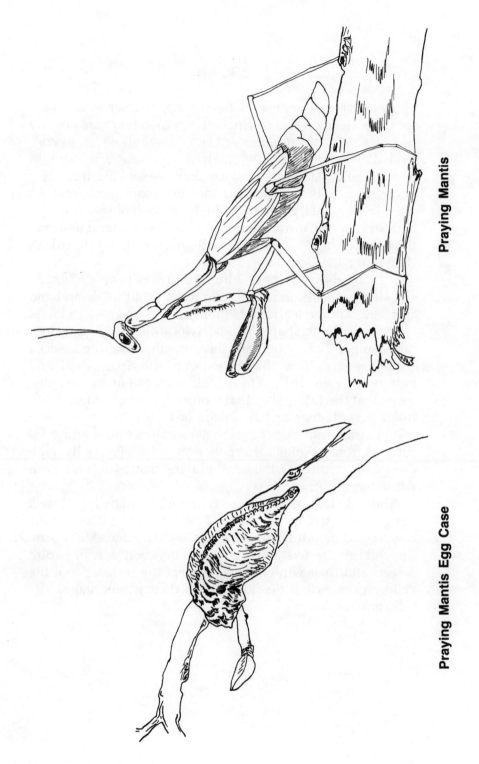

Praying Mantis

Praying Mantis Egg Case

BROWN

Most children find insects fascinating. Winter is an ideal season to develop that fascination. For then there are not any bees, hornets, mosquitoes, or black flies with which to contend. Before you take the children exploring, they should have an understanding of what they are looking for.

We, as adults, have heard the metamorphosis story so often in elementary school, in high school biology, and perhaps in college natural science courses that we tend to forget the wonder of it. But imagine discovering this miraculous change for the first time!

Begin by showing the children pictures of people at different stages of life: infancy, childhood, adulthood, and old age. The children learn that while humans do grow and look older, their basic shape—trunk, two arms, two legs—does not change. Then, compare this growth using the insect's sequence cards (see the sections on ants [page 169] and butterflies [page 161]). Enjoy their amazement as they discover that the caterpillar, that wormy sort of creature, eventually gets six legs and two pairs of wings!

If possible, experience real metamorphosis by sending for cocoons from a biological supply house. Familiarize the children with pictures of the adult praying mantis and an adult white-faced hornet.

Where do insects go in winter? Sing the following "Insect Song." As you sing about each insect, show a picture of the corresponding adult as well as its winter stage. Make sure the children understand the connection between the adult insects and their winter forms. Repeat the songs. See if the children can match the adults with their winter stage.

Strum autoharp:

Where have they gone? (F)
When did they go? (B^b)
Where are the insects? (C^7)
We want to know. (F)

It got cold outside
And many of them died.
But they left a few
To carry on the tribe.

See praying mantis,
So big and green.
See praying mantis,
She looks so serene.

The female starts to roam,
Looking for a home,
To lay her little eggs
Inside a case of foam.

White-faced hornet
Built such a nest
During the winter,
The queen wants to rest.

When the leaves are gone
It is easy to see
Bark-beetle tunnels
Etched in a tree.

Hanging from a shrub
Or decorating an oak,
Smooth tan galls
Are home to waspy folk.

Where have they gone?
When did they go?
Where are the insects?
We want to know.

It got cold outside
Any many of them died.
But they left a few
To carry on the tribe.

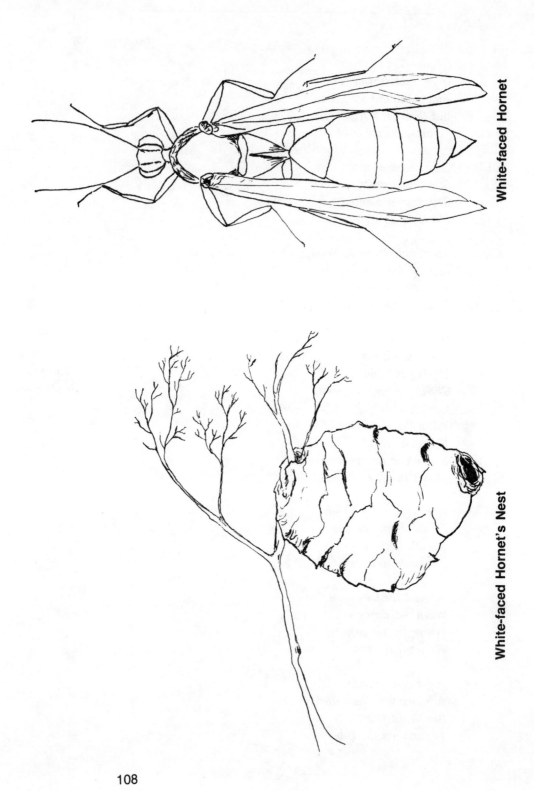

White-faced Hornet

White-faced Hornet's Nest

108

Allow the children to touch the gall, the hornet's nest, the bark, and the egg cases. Discuss differences in texture, color, and shape. When the children are familiar with these objects, go outside and show them where to find them.

This lesson requires a lot of preparation, but once the children know what they are looking for and where to look, stand back! Those three- and four-year-old eyes, so much sharper than those of adults, enable them to find scores of galls and egg cases. They will also discover brown oak leaves and twigs with tiny insect-eaten holes. Collect a few galls, some bark, and gypsy moth cocoons. Classify them according to shape. Note that they are different shades of brown.

SKUNK CABBAGE

Around the first week in March, most people are heartily sick of winter, rather depressed, and desperately in need of a cheerful note.

Fortunately, nature provides us with that hope. Walk to a low, wet spot and discover the little purple hoods nestled among the dry leaves and bits of old snow.

No, these are not discarded gnome hats, but rather the unique protection for the first flower of spring. Feel the thick waterproof hood with its narrow opening, which lets in just

Skunk Cabbage

enough light and cold air. You will see tiny yellow flowers scattered over a thick stem. Take a deep whiff of these early flowers and you will know at once why they are called skunk cabbage. *Phew!* This odor attracts early emerging insects searching for pollen, who in turn help the process of fertilizing the plant. Later, the cabbagelike leaves emerge.

PURPLE

Purple! How children like purple! It's fun to look at and it's fun to say. PURPLE!

Read "What is Purple" from *Hailstones and Halibut Bones* (see Resources). Demonstrate how purple is made from red and blue by using color paddles.

Mix red and blue fabric dyes, following package instructions, and dye some old sheets or the children's old T-shirts.

Using a flannel board with a rabbit puppet, dramatize a story about the discovery of skunk cabbage, the first spring flower. The Thornton Burgess story, "Peter Rabbit Finds Signs of Spring," is a good one to adapt (see Resources). In this story, the Merry Little Breezes urge Peter to look for the flower that blooms while the ground is still frozen. He searches the Old Briar-patch, the Green Meadow, and the Forest. Finally, he comes to a spring near the Laughing Brook and there, using his nose, discovers these mysterious flowers.

Walk outdoors to a wet, swampy area. Point out one skunk cabbage hood to the children. Encourage them to feel the thick protective hood and to smell the flowers. Then see what they can find. The response is exciting. The children get very enthusiastic as they discover one hood after another. They truly enjoy finding the hoods and will spend a long time searching for them. Although the name "skunk cabbage" may escape their memory, they never forget that exciting hunt for the little purple hoods.

When the sheets or T-shirts are dry, outline a skunk cabbage on each one, or let the children do that using a skunk cabbage template. Using fabric pens or crayons, the children

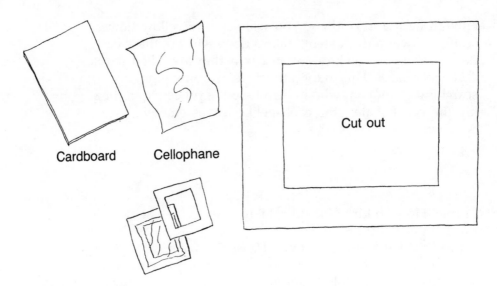

Cardboard   Cellophane

Cut out

Color Paddles

1. Following the pattern above, cut out two cardboard squares.
2. Staple red cellophane over one and blue cellophane over the other.

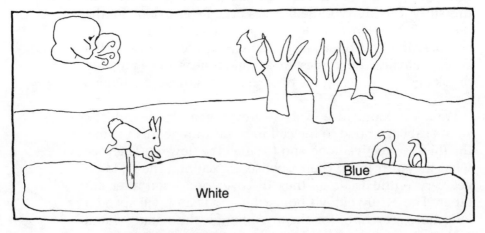

Blue

White

Peter Rabbit Story

1. Cut out the felt pieces.
2. Arrange on flannel board as shown.
3. Make Peter "hop" to the skunk cabbages.

Rabbit Pattern

1. Cut rabbit pattern out of brown paper.
2. Glue on a cotton tail.
3. Glue craft stick on back to use as a handle.

Cut these from felt.

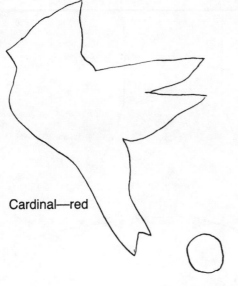

Cardinal—red

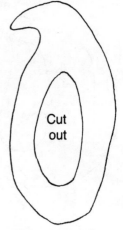

Cut out

Skunk cabbage
flower—yellow

Skunk cabbage
inside—green

Skunk cabbage
hood—purple

Cut these from felt.

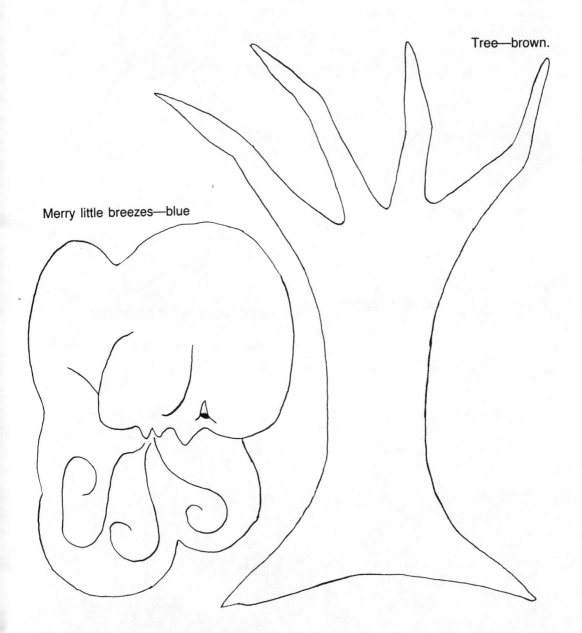

Tree—brown.

Merry little breezes—blue

can fill in the shape. You can also use the skunk cabbage pattern to make purple sewing cards for the children to stitch around the skunk cabbage shape. For these, punch holes around the edge of the pattern and thread long shoelaces through the holes.

Sing the "Skunk Cabbage" song with these autoharp chords:

Walking through the woods (D^m–A^m)
On a cold March day, (D^m–E^m)
Looking for Spring (D^m–A^m)
To come my way. (D^m–E^m)
Oh—where is Spring? (D^m)

Through the wet
Ground we stomp,
Coming to a place
We call a swamp.
Oh—where is Spring?

Here is a wet spot
Deep in the woods.
Up pop some funny
Little pointed hoods.
Oh—is this Spring?

What is this plant?
Can you tell?
What is this plant
With the terrible smell?
Oh—is this Spring?

Walking through the woods
On a cold March day,
We found Spring
In a smelly, smelly way.
Oh—here is Spring!

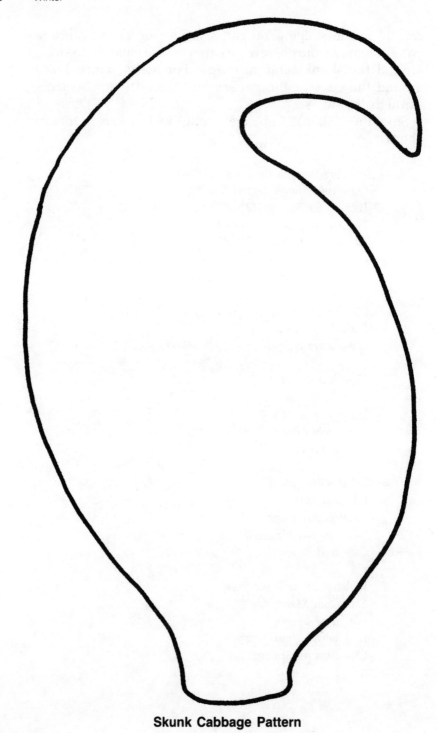

Skunk Cabbage Pattern

RAINBOW

Celebrate the vernal equinox, the first day of spring, with rainbows! The children walk into a classroom filled with color. Perched on every windowsill is a prism (see Resources). Rainbows glow on walls, chairs, and the floor. Children enjoy moving the prisms to suit their colorful fancy. As the day wears on, they shout with astonishment as the rainbows glide around the room.

The colors of winter are also arranged around the room: the cardinal puppet, the white casts of tracks, some branches of evergreen, a gall, a skunk cabbage hood, a shadow drawing.

Pass out paint chips (samples of paint colors available from any lumber, hardware, or paint store). Go outside and match the paint chips to the colors of nature. The children will find their colorful old winter friends as well as the new colors of emerging spring.

Read *A Rainbow of My Own* by Don Freeman (see Resources). The children can make a mosaic rainbow.

Snack on rainbow cookies (from *I Can Make a Rainbow* by Marjorie Frank; see Resources) or colored cubes of fruit-flavored gelatin.

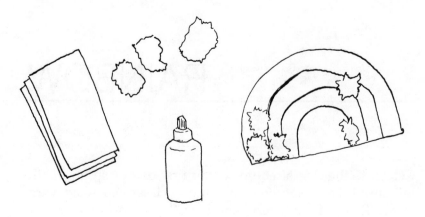

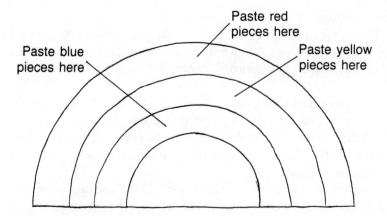

Paste blue pieces here

Paste red pieces here

Paste yellow pieces here

Mosaic Rainbow

Have ready pieces of red, yellow, and blue construction paper. Let children tear the paper into small shapes and paste on a mosaic rainbow.

SPRING

Sequencing

In early childhood education, there is an abundance of material on sequencing. The term *sequencing* is jargon for "what comes next." The literature is chock-full of rationales for teaching sequencing and for why teaching sequencing develops a child's ability to think, to reason, and to draw conclusions. It is a precursor for all sorts of academic endeavors, such as reading, science, and math.

All of this is true. All these reasons form the basis for the inclusion of sequencing activities in this book. But there is a more fundamental reason: a *need* for sequencing. According to my old *American College Dictionary*, one definition of sequencing is "a continuous or connected series." Spring is the time to make those connections. For then there is concrete evidence that green follows gray, noise follows silence, life follows death. There is a sense of comfort to continuity, to connections. Preschool sequencing activities are downright fun! They also provide comfort, stability, and unchanging expectations to today's child, who sorely needs them in this chaotic world.

Skunk Cabbage

It's freezing. Nothing doing
but a rattle of grass in the bog,
and in the sheep shed
mothermumbling deep in the throat. Two lambs,
still orange with birth.

The mother is busy licking the larger, butting her
toward a teat, paying no attention to the runt,
who is off in a corner
giving up.

It's all quite peaceful, if you like, this death.
The mother wants it, so does the lamb.

Already the ewe is digging a grave
as she licks and butts,
is scratching a trough in which to nudge a thing
that didn't work out.

I rub the lamb angrily. He has no right.
I run his legs,
force his mouth against a teat,
knead his neck to start the swallowing,

and force the milk down his lungs.
It dribbles slowly out,
and from the nose, small bubbles, unbroken.

It's all an act. I tell the legs to kick,
the eyes to look lively. They don't,
they mean it.

* * * *

Digging a grave by the bog,
small mouths of muck at work on the shovel,
down I go. Any death's my own.

And up from the roots,
like yellow-spotted purple bores of spiral leaf
to come, a sharp sour scent

muscles in,
says, Live, God damn you, live.

By   Rennie McQuilkin

DEATH AND DECAY

Teach death and decay in spring? A time when new buds and green are just emerging? A time when, after the rigors of winter, we need hope and life?

Here on the goat farm spring is just that—a time of hope and life, and a time of death and decay. On the one hand, the goat yard is filled with the skipping, prancing kids. Newly born fuzzy coats are so soft! Pick a kid up and it nuzzles your face. The kids team up and race across the yard, up the rock pile. We perch on stones in the goat yard and laugh out loud at their antics. Curious, they literally hop, skip, and jump over to sniff us, chew on our shoelaces, and curl up in our laps in the sun. And as you hold one close, the pain recedes. The pain caused by the death of the kid who didn't make it.

Those who die are buried in the south lot under the pines, their bodies nourishing the soil. I plant daffodils there.

LESSON

At the close of a parent-child session, a mother came up to me in tears. "Marcia," she said, "could you please do a program on death?" Her mother was dying and she just could not discuss it with her preschooler. I glibly replied, "Sure," and it was only later when I sat down that I began to have qualms. Generally, we Americans do not cope at all well with death. We tend to ignore it, or talk around it, or isolate it. We have forgotten the ancient wisdom that death is indeed a natural part of the cycle of existence.

And death should be presented as such to a small child.

122

Spring is a good time to start because the continuity of life is so evident. Small children can see and feel and smell the life that has been brought forth from death.

Use the following sequence cards of acorn to decaying log to explain the cycle of existence. On succeeding days, discuss each stage of the cycle.

Day 1 Collect acorns, find sprouted acorns. Bring some in to sprout.

Day 2 Visit some oak saplings (young trees).

Day 3 Visit a healthy, mature oak.

Day 4 Visit a dying, or dead, tree.

Day 5 Visit a rotting log.

Encourage children to look carefully at each stage and to describe what they see. You may need to guide the discussions and supply essential words: "Yes, the acorn has *sprouted*. See the roots." Explore the young and mature trees thoroughly (for hints, see the section on oaks, page 195). When you visit the dying tree, look for dead branches with no leaves, look for insects, and for bird's nests. Note all the uses nature makes of a dying tree as it provides food for some and homes for others.

Standing dead trees are called *snags*. Snags make good homes for birds who need to nest in holes. A chickadee pair, for example, nests in the dying pear tree in my front yard.

Small children love to explore rotting logs. These provide a great opportunity to touch. The composting wood is soft and moist. Careful exploration will reveal snails, a salamander or two, and insects. Insects such as carpenter ants, termites, sow bugs and millipedes feed on decaying logs. Look also for small sprouting plants. Moss and ferns grow in decaying logs. Worms live there, too. Worms! Young children are fascinated with these creatures that eat soil and enrich the surrounding earth with their castings.

This cycle of acorn to rotting log illustrates the natural cycle of existence of which death is only one part. When you talk about the dying tree and rotting log, don't be afraid to use the words *dying* and *death*. Use them naturally, just as you would say "sprouting."

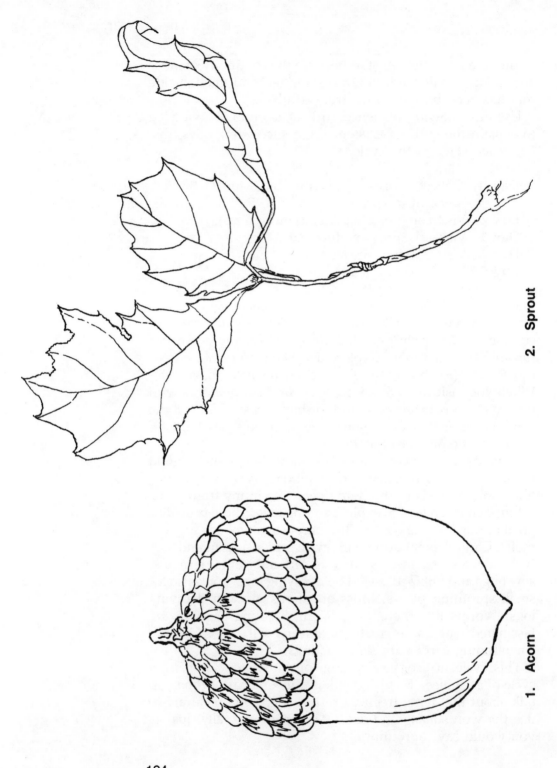

2. Sprout

1. Acorn

124

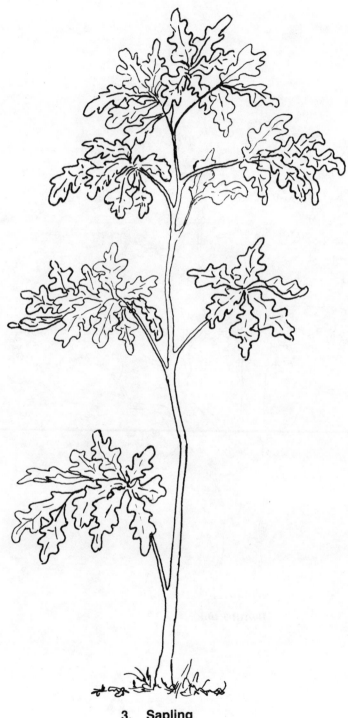

3. Sapling

125

4. Mature oak

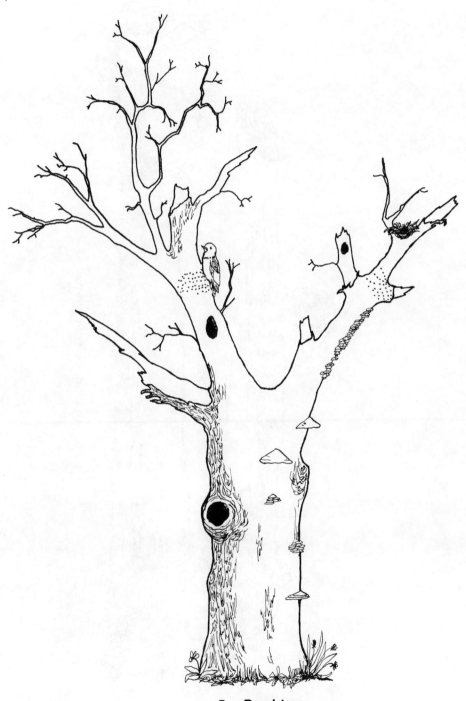

5. Dead tree

6. Rotting log with plants

128

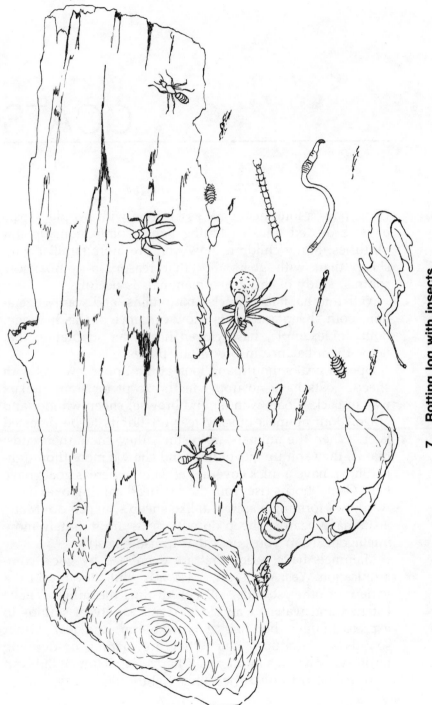

7. Rotting log with insects

GOATS

Goats have a long history of association with people. Goats have provided milk, clothing, and companionship for centuries. Many children, however, are more familiar with sheep than with goats. For that reason, a comparison/contrast study of these two mammals is useful.

Native to habitats of rocks, mountains, and scant vegetation, both sheep and goats show evidence of this heritage. Both, for example, have cloven hoofs, an adaptation that helps them balance in precarious places.

Open a goat's mouth and look at the upper jaw. As with sheep, goats have no upper teeth except for some molars way in back. Goats wander and browse; sheep wander and graze. Both animals quickly tear off tidbits to be digested later. When the animals are resting, they chew their cuds; that is, they spit up bits of food and chew it more thoroughly. Sheep have a thick covering of wool, whereas goats have hair. Goats' horns rise from the forehead curving over backward, not forming a spiral, unlike sheep's, which do. Many goats have beards; sheep do not. Goats are infinitely more intelligent. (Can you guess that I raise goats!)

Mammals have needs that are expressed by vocal communication. Yes, goats say "*Maaaaaa.*" But they produce a variety of other sounds, all with distinct meanings. I have listened and watched my goats use a variety of sounds to express hunger, bonding at birth, alarm, and fear. Other sounds are produced when they are mating, or defining territory, or when a mother calls her young. Human kids can learn to listen to hear the things nature has to say.

LESSON

Goats' natural breeding cycle starts in the fall. Does come into heat after the first sharp frost in October. As the gestation period is five months, this means that kids start to arrive in March. If you are fortunate enough to have field trip funds, visit a 'dairy goat farm in your vicinity. If not, goat owners are especially eager to bring their livestock into the classroom. For a list of goat owners near you, write to the American Dairy Goat Association (see Resources).

Before the animal arrives, caution children not to startle it with loud noises. Speak softly and the children will imitate your behavior. Allow the children plenty of time to explore the animal by touching it gently. Now is a good time to learn to pet an animal by stroking with, not against, the grain of the fur.

Running Kid

Compare goat body parts to human body parts: "Let's count the legs: one-two-three-four. How many legs do you have? One-two. Show me your ears. Are your ears larger or smaller than the goat's ears? Open your eyes *wide*. Look at the person next to you. See the round black pupil in the eye? Now look at the goat's eye. The pupil is rectangular! Show me your teeth. See, the goat doesn't have any top teeth except way in back. Where is your hair? Feel the goat's hair."

At a Head Start workshop in Nebraska, we arranged for both a goat and a sheep to make an appearance. The teachers delighted in discovering differences between these two mammals: hair versus wool, the curious versus the placid nature. The similarities are easily observable to a pre-schooler: both have cloven hoofs, both are ruminants and therefore chew their cuds. Contrast the uses of the animals: sheep are raised for wool, goats for milk. (Yes, there are angora goats, and people do milk sheep, but it's best to stick to generalities.) Both animals are raised for meat.

If your exhibit animal is a milking doe, ask the owner to give a milking demonstration. Perhaps she will also let each child try to milk.

Sequence cards can be made for the life cycle of the goat. The kid is the baby, growing into a yearling. The adult female is called a doe, the male, a buck. Castrated males are called wethers; these are often the goat pets.

Use the sequencing cards to illustrate the process of "grain to cheese."

Ricki and Robert Carroll give cheesemaking workshops in the kitchen of their Victorian home, nestled up against the Berkshires. The Carrolls are co-owners of the New England Cheesemaking Supply Company. Try making this ricotta cheese using a recipe from their book, *Cheesemaking Made Easy* (see Resources). It is easy and, best of all for young children, the results are immediate.

Buy one gallon of goat's milk from a goat owner or from a nearby natural-foods store. Warm one gallon of whole goat's milk to 206°F. Stir in ¼ cup cider vinegar. The milk will rapidly coagulate. I let it sit anywhere from 15 minutes to ½ hour. Then drain the curd into a cheesecloth-lined colander.

1.   Kid

2.   Yearling

3.   Adult doe

1.   Goat eating grass

2.   Milking the goat

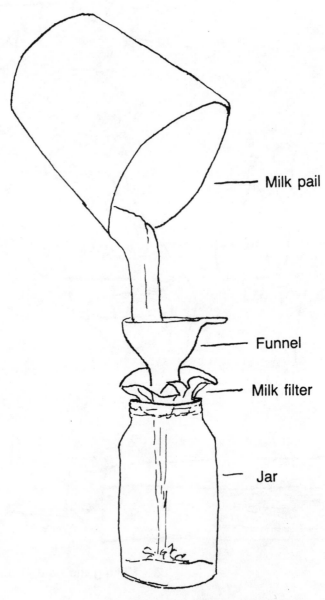

Milk pail

Funnel

Milk filter

Jar

3. Straining the milk

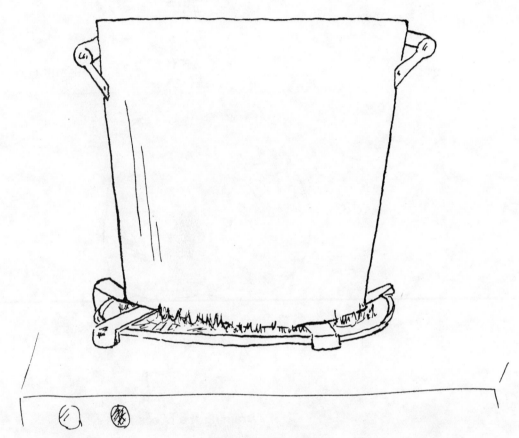

4.   Warming the milk

5.   Draining the cheese

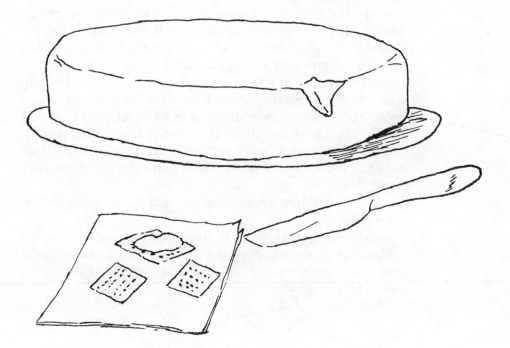

6. Cheese!

Drain for one minute. Place the curds in a bowl. Mix 3 tablespoons melted butter and ½ teaspoon baking soda into the curd. Mix in thoroughly. Place the cheese in a container, cover, and refrigerate it until ready for use. This cheese, write the Carrolls, is excellent for cooking. And it is so delicious! It makes a great lasagna. It's also delicious mixed with herbs and spread on crackers.

Study the different sounds the human voice can make. Assign adjectives to these sounds: loud, soft, angry, happy. Listen to songs, poetry, stories, and nursery rhymes with strong rhythms and sounds. Discuss different uses of the human voice. Learn other mammal sounds. Record the farm visit on tape. Listen to recordings of animal noises. Read books about animal sounds. Sing "Old MacDonald" and "I Bought Me a Rooster" (there is a host of animal folk songs). Play musical games, such as "Here Stands a Redbird" (see page 63), changing the word *redbird* to the desired mammal's name.

Have the children imitate sounds and act like the appropriate mammal.

Match mammal pictures to the correct sounds.

Make instruments. Play them randomly, in rhythm, or with vocal accompaniment. Make up songs about animal noises and sing with the instruments.

FROGS AND TOADS

It's on one of those late-night trips to the barn to check on the birth of a kid that I suddenly hear the true sign of spring: Peepers! Until that magical night, the woods are silent in the long winter dark. Now, even though we still get snowstorms and freezing temperatures, the change toward spring is evident. There is noise—life!—at night. In our swamp, the wood frogs sing; this is the first stage in these amphibians' life cycle.

In 1735, Carolus Linnaeus devised the classification of animals, including *amphibians*. The name literally means "double lives," for these animals spend periods of their lives on land and other periods in water. Frogs, toads, newts, and salamanders are all amphibians. Other characteristics of amphibians include the following:

1. Their immature stages are spent in or near water. The young are called tadpoles.
2. The skin is porous and moist, and assists in breathing.
3. They emit sounds by forcibly expelling air from the lungs.
4. They are cold blooded.
5. They do not drink but absorb moisture through the skin.

The following are specific characteristics of toads:

1. Their life cycle consists of egg, tadpole, and adult stages.

2. They have "warts" (no, you can't get warts from touching a toad, although you could get a slight rash). These warts are glands, which secrete a substance disagreeable for any animal seeking toad dinners. The large bumps just behind the ear are the parotid glands.
3. The eyes bulge when open. They flatten when closed and help push food down.
4. The nose consists of two tiny nostrils.
5. The ears are flat; they are the oval spots behind each eye. They are really the eardrums, since there is no external ear like ours.
6. The mouth is wide; the jaws are horny. Toads do not have teeth; they swallow prey whole.
7. The strong hind legs help in jumping. Also, toads dig with these.
8. The tongue is attached at the front and is covered with a sticky substance.
9. Toads feed on vegetable matter as tadpoles. As adults, they eat insects.
10. For protection, toads burrow into the earth. Their earthen color provides camouflage from enemies.
11. Toads are the gardener's friends because they eat insects. Also, it is pleasant for both toad and gardener to stop work for a while and scratch the toad's back.

Toads and frogs are similar and are often confused. Here are two lists to help you distinguish between them.

Similarities of Toads and Frogs
1. Both are amphibians.
2. Both have the same general shape.
3. Both have bulging eyes.
4. Both have long back legs and shorter front legs.
5. Both eat insects as adults.
6. Both have a life cycle consisting of egg, tadpole, and adult stages.

Differences Between Toads and Frogs

1. Toads have rough and bumpy skin.
2. Toads' eggs are laid in strings.
3. Toads hibernate in the ground.
4. Generally, toads feed at night.
5. Toads are friendlier to children.
6. Children will most likely find toads in dry earth.

1. Frog skins are smooth and shiny.
2. Frogs' eggs are laid in masses.
3. Many frogs hibernate in mud and ponds.
4. Generally, frogs feed by day.
5. Frogs couldn't care less about children.
6. Children will most likely find frogs in moist, or wet, areas.

LESSON

First thing in the morning, play "The Frog Pond" (see Resources) on the record player. As the children arrive, they will excitedly listen and try to figure out the sounds. Show a picture of the male frog with his throat puffed out. If you have been able to find some frog eggs, or have ordered them through a biological supply house, show them. Let the children gently touch the protective jelly surrounding the eggs. Present the sequence cards.

Bring a toad into the classroom. Allow children to touch it gently. Make sure they wash their hands after handling—a very few children get rashes from toads. Place the toad on a large sheet of plastic. Allow the children to watch it move, breathe, and eat. Discuss its body parts. Compare its body parts with theirs.

Visit a toad habitat. A nearby patch of dirt with a few plants for cover will do. Even though you may not find a toad, point out likely places where it would hide. Encourage children to move as toads do and to find their own toady hiding spots.

Repeat the above activities with a frog, available from a biological supply house (see Resources) if you do not have access to neighborhood frogs. Note: frogs are harder to hold.

Male Frog Singing

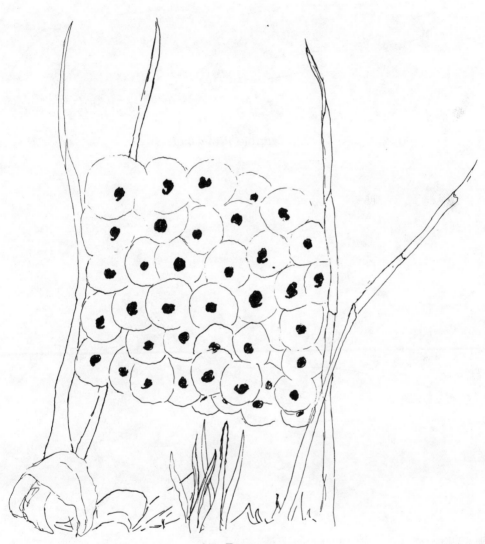

1.   **Frog eggs**

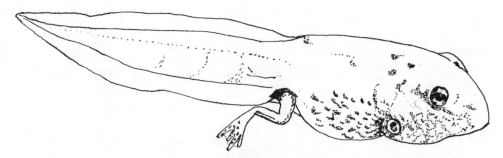

2.   Tadpole first stage

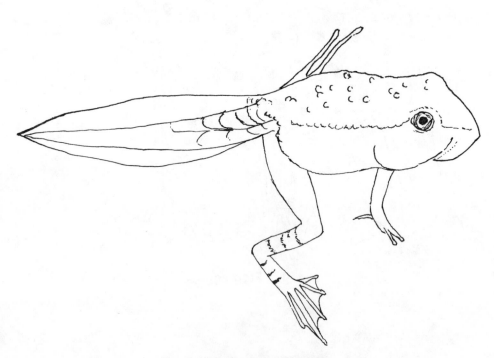

3.   Tadpole second stage

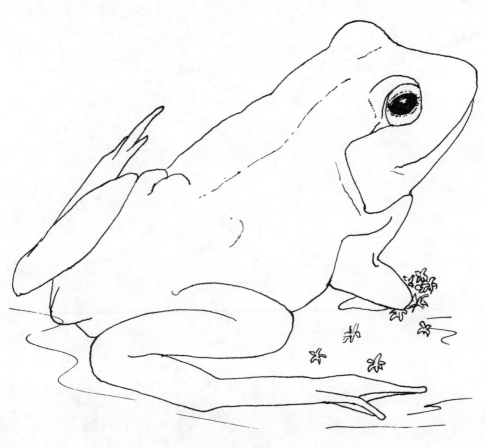

4. **Adult frog**

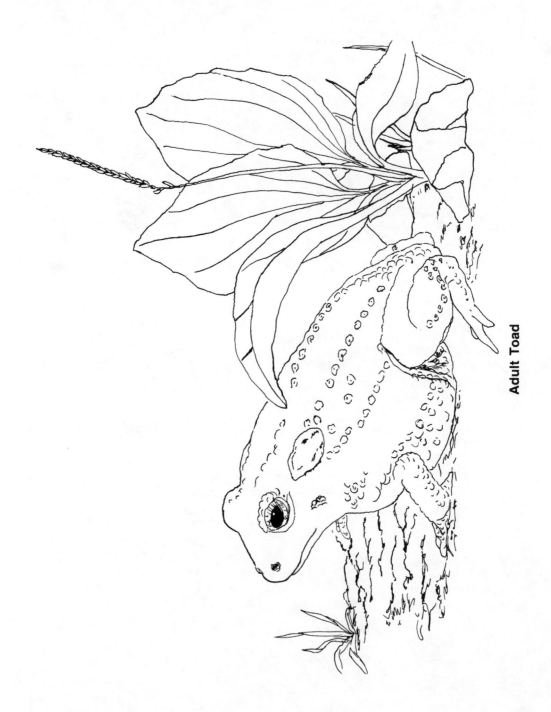

Adult Toad

They slip away easily and hop faster. They are not as friendly as toads. For these reasons, keep frogs in large see-through containers that are escape-proof.

Have both a frog and a toad available in the classroom. Take the time to compare and contrast the two. Encourage the children to discover their likenesses and differences.

Read picture books about frogs and toads, such as Arnold Lobel's *Frog and Toad* series (see Resources).

Sing and read frog songs, such as "Froggie Went a-Courtin' " (see Resources).

Sing about and act out the life cycles of frogs and toads.

Make frogs out of green construction paper and toads out of sandpaper. Have the children classify them according to texture and color. Match to the correct environment.

Play the frog number game.

Listen to recordings of frog and toad sounds. Play "toadical chairs" to the music.

Put the letter *F* on frog pictures, the letter *T* on toad pictures. Have the children trace the letters.

Make and eat toad pretzels.

Toad Pretzels

1½ cups warm water
1 package dry yeast
4 cups flour
1 teaspoon sugar
1 teaspoon salt
1 egg, lightly beaten with 1 tablespoon water

Dissolve the yeast in the water in a large bowl. Mix the flour, sugar, and salt in a second bowl. With a large spoon, work the flour mixture into the yeast mixture. When about 3 cups of flour mix have been worked in, begin to knead the mixture on a counter top. Keep adding the remaining flour mix, working it into the dough. Give each child a portion of dough. Shape the dough into toads. Place onto greased pans. Paint with egg-water mixture. Bake 25 minutes or until golden brown at 425°F. Makes about 25 toads.

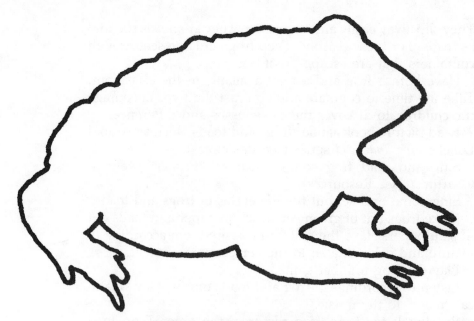

Pattern for Sandpaper Toad—Make Ten

Pattern for Construction Paper Frog—Make Ten

Frog and Toad Environment Game

1. Make frog environment from pieces of construction paper and turtle sticker.
2. Cover with clear plastic.
3. Make toad environment from bumpy cardboard and magazine vegetable pictures.
4. Have children match the sandpaper toad and green construction paper frog to the correct environment, using touch as a clue, i.e., smooth frog to smooth environment.

Frog Number Game

1. Using the construction paper frog pattern, make five more frogs from green construction paper.
2. On the first frog place one big dot on one side with a magic marker.
3. On the other side write the numeral 1.
4. On the second frog make two spots and the numeral 2.
5. Continue up to number five.
6. Out of construction paper make a pond with one lily pad. Continue up to number five.

Children must match the correct frog to the lily pad using either dots or numerals.

Use the picture above as a guide.

EGGS

Sometimes, before I show frog eggs to children, I hand them a hard-boiled chicken egg. They can feel the hard shell and even peel it off. Then we compare the chicken's egg to the frog eggs. This creates great wonderment that *both* are eggs!

Members of every group of animals lay eggs. Some are laid in nests on land, others are deposited in water, and still others are protected inside the adult's body. All eggs are protected from predators, but the methods vary. Some, as in mammals, are inside the adult's body, as mentioned. Others are laid in protective nests of twigs and mud. The color of the egg may serve as camouflage from its enemies. Some eggs, like those of frogs, are covered in a protective jelly.

For most birds, the production of an egg takes about twenty-four hours. Once fertilized, the egg moves down the oviduct. At the end of the oviduct, it receives a shell. Shells have many tiny openings, which permit air to reach the embryo. The shape of the egg is dependent on the nest. If pointed at one end, the egg is generally that of a cliff or ground dweller. If pushed, these pointy eggs will not roll out of the nest, but will roll in a circle instead. If the eggs are round, they are generally that of a tree or cavity nester. There is no place for them to roll!

Many naturalists believe that the eggs' colors are a protective device. Ground nesters often have spotted eggs that blend in with the area around the nest. Birds that nest in bushes and trees often have pale blue or green eggs, which are less visible in the dappled light of the trees. Eggs laid in dark holes are often white so that they are easily seen by the parents. Eggshell texture varies, too. Small birds' eggs are most often smoother than a hen's egg, for example.

155

Egg sizes range from the tiny half-inch egg of the hummingbird to the eight-inch ostrich egg.

The term "clutch" refers to the number of eggs in one nest.

There are many differences between the eggs of birds, reptiles, amphibians, insects, and fish. While birds lay hard-shelled eggs, reptiles lay eggs with a leathery surface. Frogs, on the other hand, lay eggs covered with a soft, jellylike covering. Birds lay from one to twenty eggs, depending on the species. Amphibians and reptiles lay anywhere from ten eggs to hundreds of eggs. Insects and fish lay eggs in the thousands.

In addition, birds care for their young. They use their bodies to keep the eggs warm. They feed their young. They encourage them to learn to fly or to swim. Many reptile, amphibian, and insect parents never see their young; they lay the eggs and leave.

LESSON

Many nursery schools borrow an incubator and hatch hen eggs in the spring. The children eagerly await that first chick's hatching. If you decide to do this, make sure you have a responsible home for the hatched chickens. A less expensive, but equally dramatic, activity is to collect, or order, frog, toad, or salamander eggs. Keep them in water and watch the metamorphosis from egg to tadpole. Make sure there are not too many eggs or they will die of oxygen starvation. As the water evaporates, I add to it water from the same swamp or pond from which I collected the eggs.

Children thoroughly enjoy watching the above two activities. Make a chart or graph of the development.

Contrast and compare the different kinds of eggs, using the real eggs and/or pictures of them.

Use the sequence cards "eggs to adult."

Play the egg texture game.

Read Ruth Heller's picture book, *Chickens Aren't the Only Ones* (see Resources).

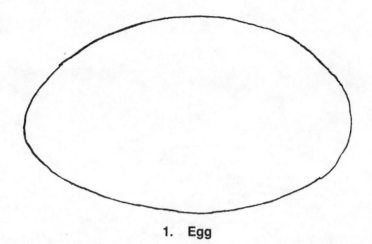

1.   Egg

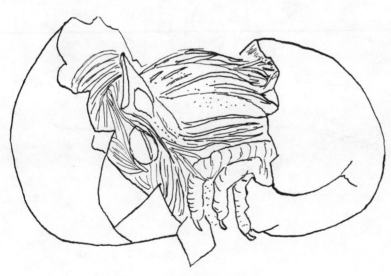

2.   Emerging chick

3.   Young bird (fledgling)

4. Adult Blue Jay

Egg Texture Game

1. Use magazine photographs of a bird, turtle, and frog. Glue onto three different poster boards.
2. Next to the bird picture glue a large egg shape made out of shelf paper, shiny side up.
3. Next to the frog picture glue some bubbly packing plastic cut in an egg shape.
4. Next to the turtle glue a thin sheet of styrofoam in an egg shape.
5. Cut out the letters e-g-g in each material (shelf paper; packing material; styrofoam).
6. Glue the letters to poster board.
7. Have the children match the word "egg" to the picture, using texture as the clue.

BUTTERFLIES AND MOTHS

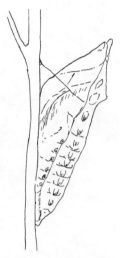

Butterflies and moths also start life as eggs! They certainly go through some dramatic changes on their way to adulthood. Both are members of the order Lepidoptera, meaning "scaly wings." Both are insects with three body parts, six legs, and two sets of wings. Both undergo complete metamorphosis from egg to larva to pupa to adult.

There are distinct differences between the two.

Butterflies fly by day, rest with their wings erect, have thin antennae with swollen tips, have a thin body, and only a few of them are destructive. A butterfly larva attaches itself to a firm support before changing into the naked pupa, known as a chrysalis. Butterflies emerge quickly from the chrysalis.

Moths, on the other hand, fly at night, rest with their wings held flat, have a plump and furry body, have feathery antennae, and many of them are pests. Moth larvae burrow into the ground and or into dead leaves or grass on the ground in order to pupate. Others spin a cocoon within which to pupate, or use leaves as the outer layer. Moths take a longer time to emerge as adults.

Butterfly Chrysalis

LESSON

You can either collect pupae from your yard or order them from a biological supply house. When the adult emerges, its wings are wet. It needs enough space to spread these wings fully to dry. Otherwise, it will dry in a deformed shape, crippling the insect. So make sure your container is large enough.

Moth Cocoon

161

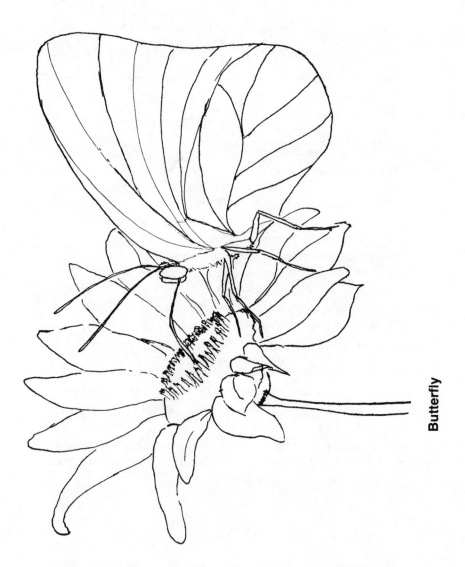

Butterfly

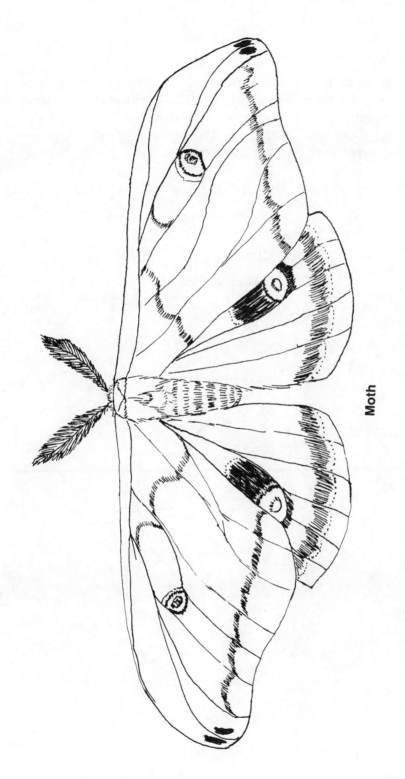

Moth

163

Look at the illustrations of the butterflies and moths. Count the four wings. Say, "This butterfly did not always look this beautiful. In fact, when it was a baby, it looked quite different." Then show the sequence cards. Have the children use them. Use this finger play:

Little crawly caterpillar (Fingers crawl up arm)
Onto a leaf will creep
He'll make himself a chrysalis (Make a fist)
And then go fast asleep
Wakes up by and by (Spread fingers)
To find he has become a beautiful butterfly.
(Hold fingers wide and flutter)

1.   **Butterfly egg**

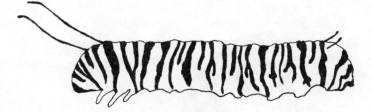

2.   Caterpillar

3.   Chrysalis

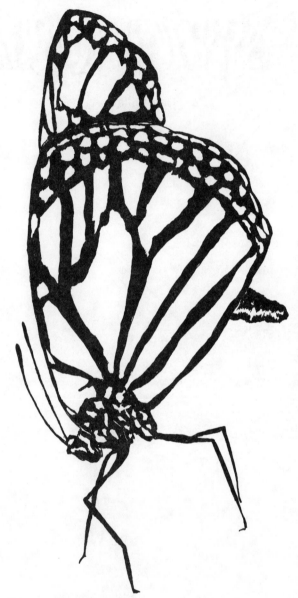

4. Adult monarch butterfly

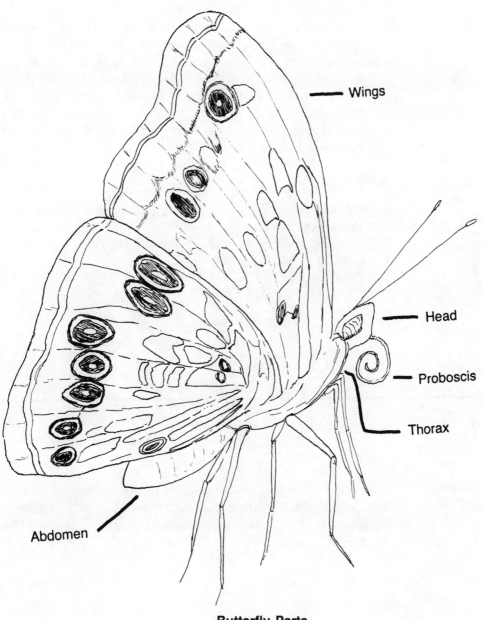

Wings

Head

Proboscis

Thorax

Abdomen

Butterfly Parts

Blindfold a child. Have him walk to a designated place. He will most likely put out his hands to feel his way. Point to the antennae on the insect picture and mention that they are used as a sense organ just as the child used his hands.

Using the illustration on page 167, point out the body parts of the butterfly: the head, the thorax, the abdomen, the wings, the proboscis. The proboscis is used as a straw to suck up nectar from the blossoms. Center the discussion on the proboscis.

Butterfly Wings

1. Cut grocery bag down one side, cut out bottom, spread out lengthwise.
2. Have children color or paint designs on the bags.
3. Cut slits in "wings" as shown.
4. Put wings on children.

Butterfly Nectar

1 banana slice
1 strawberry
1 cup milk
Mix everything in a blender.
This recipe makes one serving.

5. Have the children "fly" over to the flower cups and sip nectar with a straw.

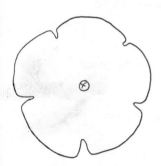

Flower Pattern
for Top of Cup

Make grocery-bag wings and fly to the butterfly nectar in the flower cup. Sip the nectar through a proboscis (a straw).

Read *The Very Hungry Caterpillar* by Eric Carle (see Resources).

ANTS

Is your preschool located in the city? And you can't find any native animals to observe? Well, there are always ants. While many adults are squeamish about ants, most children are not. In fact, they are often fascinated with them. A group of us stopped pedestrian traffic one day as we knelt in a long row over the sidewalk in front of the bank on Main Street. We dropped bits of crackers on the ground and watched with hand lenses as the ants appeared and carried the crackers away.

Like all insects, ants have three body parts: the head, the thorax, and the abdomen. They also have six legs.

With their long legs, ants can run rapidly and even leap when frightened. There are tiny hairs on an ant's leg, which it uses to comb and clean the antennae. It is important to keep the antennae clean, as these organs are vital to the ant. When ants meet, they touch and rub each other's antennae to communicate. An ant's eyes are small and practically useless. An ant, therefore, uses its antennae as a touch organ to find out where it is going. The antennae also serve as an organ for smelling. This sense of smell helps the ant with direction. It lays down a trail of formic acid, which has a definite odor. Then it follows its nose or, rather, antennae, home. Formic acid is also used for defense against enemies, as it is an irritant.

Ants are social insects, which means they work together and help each other. They even have a "social stomach." They share their food with each other. When an ant swallows food, only part of it goes to its stomach. The rest is retained in its crop, from which it can bring up small quantities to feed to others.

An ant begins life as an egg. The egg hatches into a grub, which is fed by the workers. The grub then pupates in a small, oval-shaped cocoon. Later, the adult ant emerges from the cocoon.

Each colony is comprised of a queen, winged males, and wingless, sterile females. The queen works laying eggs. These eggs are licked by the nurse ants, which prevents mold. This also causes the eggs to stick together in a packet, so they can easily be carried in times of danger. Nurse ants will carry the eggs and larvae deeper into the ground where it is cooler, if the day is too hot. They feed the larvae regurgitated food from their crops.

The food-gathering ants forage for food and share it with the rest of the colony. Other workers enlarge the nest, keep it clean, and protect it from enemies.

Remember the tale about the grasshopper and the ant? It's true; the ants do work diligently in the summer. In winter, they mass together underground to hibernate.

LESSON

Hold up this picture of the ant. Say, "An ant is an insect. An ant has three body parts: the head, the thorax, the abdomen. Let's count the body parts, one-two-three." It is not important that the children remember the names, but just that there are three body parts. "When this ant was a baby it looked like this." "What did you look like when you were a baby?"

Continue explaining, using the illustrations, the ant's life cycle. Contrast these drastic physical changes to a human's relatively undramatic growth. Make some human growth sequence cards by using pictures from magazines.

Play sequencing games with these cards. Have the children arrange them in the correct order. Take one out and have the children find where it belongs.

"Show me your legs. How many do you have? What can you do with your legs? See, an ant has legs too. It has very long legs. It can run and it can leap." Have the children run and leap like ants.

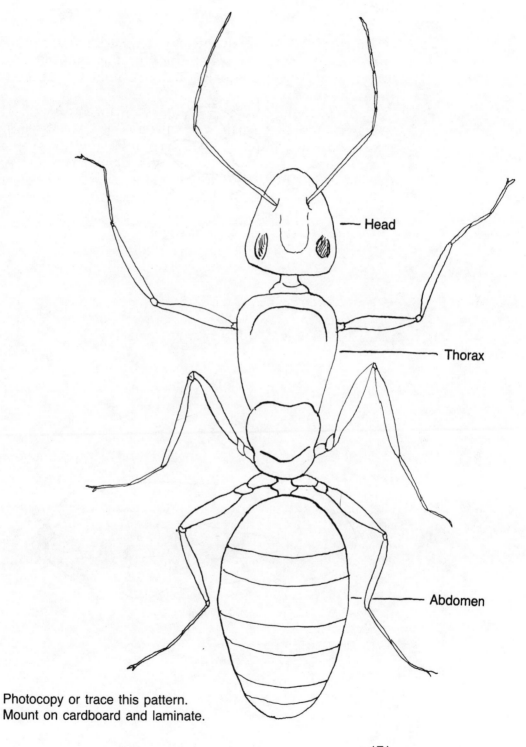

— Head

— Thorax

— Abdomen

Photocopy or trace this pattern.
Mount on cardboard and laminate.

1.   Ant eggs

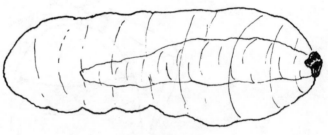

2.   Ant larva

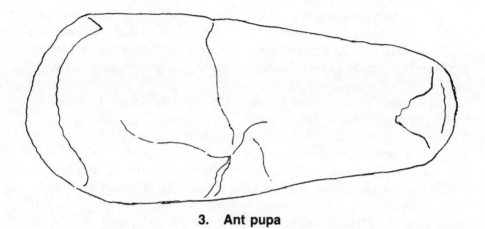

3.   Ant pupa

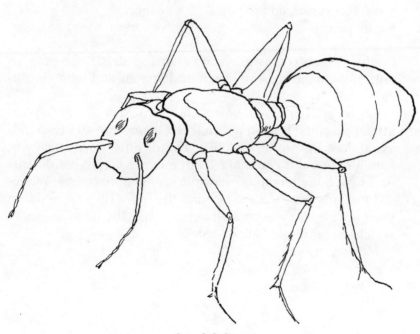

4.   Adult ant

"An ant cannot see well. How would you know where you are going if you couldn't see?" Blindfold a child and have her walk to a designated spot. The child will most likely put out her hands to feel the way. "How is Mary finding her way? Yes, by feeling with her hands. And that is just what an ant does. It feels its way. But it uses *antennae* [point to antennae on picture] to feel."

Spray some perfume. "What does your nose tell you? Yes, it smells the perfume. An ant smells. But it doesn't use its nose; it smells with its antennae! As an ant walks along, it leaves a smelly trail to follow home so it won't get lost."

"Ants are like people. People help each other. Ants help each other. The mother ant is called the queen. While the queen is laying eggs, the nurse ants watch the children. Who takes care of you while your mom works?"

Continue to make comparisons between children and ants:

Child	*Ant Eggs and Larvae*
bathed by parents	eggs are licked
protected (is helped while crossing streets, and so forth)	eggs are carried away in times of danger
fed by parents	fed regurgitated food

Say, "When you awake you yawn and stretch. So does an ant. Now stand up and yawn and stretch and let's go outside."

Go to anthills. Take some sweet cookies or crackers to attract the ants. Encourage children to observe and respond. What does the anthill look like? Do the ants move quickly or slowly? How can you make them move faster? What do ants eat? Leave the bits of cookie and see what happens. Where did the ants get the sand to build the hill? (They carried it in their jaws as they excavated below.) Use the hand lenses to watch the ants carefully.

VIOLETS AND SEEDS

Spring is a time of growth. The most astonishing growth is that of violets. No matter where I have given nature programs, I have found violets—in the woods, in suburban lawns, in pavement cracks in the city.

Their ubiquity is due in part to the ferocious nature of their seeds. The seed pods curl back, and, with force, the seeds jump away from the parent plant.

Violets

Examine a violet plant closely. Note the saw-toothed, heart-shaped leaves. These are good for crayon rubbings (see page 197 for directions). Look closely at the base of the plant. Here you will find tiny flowers, which never open. These are called cleistogamous, or seed, flowers. They are pollinated from their own anthers.

Unlike their shy seed-flower sisters, the more commonly seen blossoms of the violet are showier. They come in many colors, depending on the species, including blue, purple, white, and combinations thereof. Pick these flowers to press. Use them later to decorate bookmarks or notepaper. Or eat them! They are rich in vitamin C. Garnish a salad with violets. Make candied violets for desserts. In short, enjoy the violet!

LESSON

Start your plant studies with seeds. The night before the seed lesson, soak some large, dry lima beans (available at any grocery store). Also, bring to class fruits with seeds. Let the children cut into the fruits with table knives and discover the seeds. Contrast tiny apple seeds with large avocado seeds. Introduce the seed-part names by putting a giant lima bean seed, cut out of felt, on the flannel board.

Engage in some dramatic play acting. "We are seeds, and it is spring. It is getting warm, and we are growing. Oops! I grew so much that my coat split. Oh my! See how the

Lima Bean and Embryo Pattern

1. Cut three pieces of felt in bean pattern, one in brown, two in yellow. Brown is the seed coat, yellow are the cotyledons.
2. Cut one embryo piece in green felt.
3. Place yellow cotyledon on flannel board, put embryo on top, cover with second cotyledon.
4. Place brown (seed coat) on top. Then peel back seed coat, open cotyledon and show embryo.

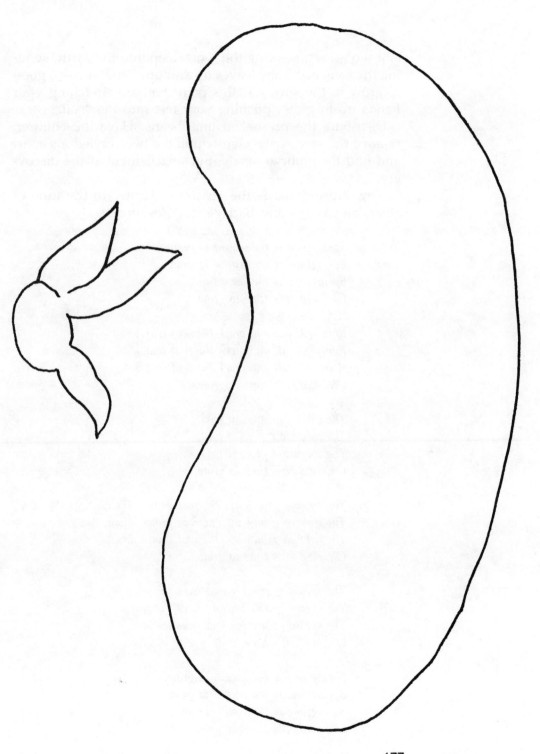

embryo grows, sending the roots deep into the earth, sending the stem and baby leaves up and up. Oh! It feels so good to grow in the sun." At this point you are stretching your hands up to grow, pushing your feet into the "soil."

Distribute the presoaked lima beans. Have the children remove the seed coats. Gently pull the two cotyledons apart and find the embryo inside. Such excitement at the discovery!

Sing "Springtime Is the Season to Grow" to the tune of "Oats and Beans and Barley" (see Resources).

> *Springtime is the season to grow,*
> *Springtime is the season to grow,*
> *Springtime is the season to grow.*
> *Oh, seed, it's time to grow.*
>
> *Rain will fall and crack the seed coat,*
> *Rain will fall and crack the seed coat,*
> *Rain will fall and crack the seed coat.*
> *Oh, seed, it's time to grow.*
>
> *The cotyledon gives it food,*
> *The cotyledon gives it food,*
> *The cotyledon gives it food.*
> *Oh, seed, it's time to grow.*
>
> *The embryo grows up, the root grows down,*
> *The embryo grows up, the root grows down,*
> *The embryo grows up, the root grows down.*
> *Oh, seed, it's time to grow.*
>
> *The sprout grows big and faces the sun,*
> *The sprout grows big and faces the sun,*
> *The sprout grows big and faces the sun.*
> *Oh, seed, it's time to grow.*
>
> *Springtime is the season to grow,*
> *Springtime is the season to grow,*
> *Springtime is the season to grow.*
> *Oh, seed, it's FUN to grow!*

Plant quick-growing radish or lettuce seeds in cups filled with potting soil. If you have the resources, plant a small garden outdoors. Contact the National Gardening Association for information. They sponsor school and community gardens. The address is The National Gardening Association, 180 Flynn Avenue, Burlington, Vermont 05401.

If you have little money and no space, sprout alfalfa seeds in a jar. It is a satisfying crop; alfalfa grows quickly and tastes good.

Use the sequence cards of growth from seed to flower.

Read Arnold Lobel's short story "The Garden" from *Frog and Toad Together* (see Resources).

Listen and then sing along with Billy B.'s "I Am a Sprout" (see Resources).

Introduce the violet plant by naming its parts: roots, stem, leaves, and flowers. Then each child can meet her own violet plant. Find the plant parts; note the shape of the leaves, the color of the petals, and the number of petals. Look for the seed flower.

Play the missing-parts game (see pages 184–188).

Do the following violet finger play:

> Five little violets growing by the door,
> A bunny ate one and then there were four.
> Four little violets smiling at me,
> I picked one and then there were three.
> Three little violets purple and blue,
> Give one to a friend and then there are two.
> Two little violets grow in the sun,
> Pick one for jelly and then there is one.
> One little violet grows all summer,
> Making seeds to start another!

Paint *v*'s with violet paint.

Talk about the seed pods that shoot out the seeds. Have the children stand together in a huddle. Ask them to try to raise their leaves (arms) to the sun and grow. There is just not enough room. Then ask them to jump away from the parent plant and see how much space there is now!

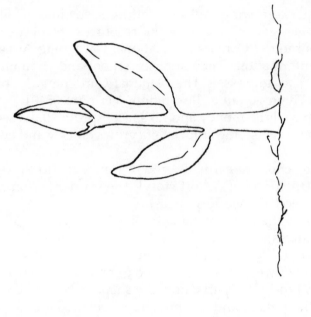

2. Seedling

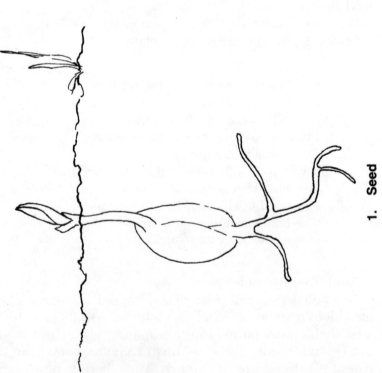

1. Seed

180

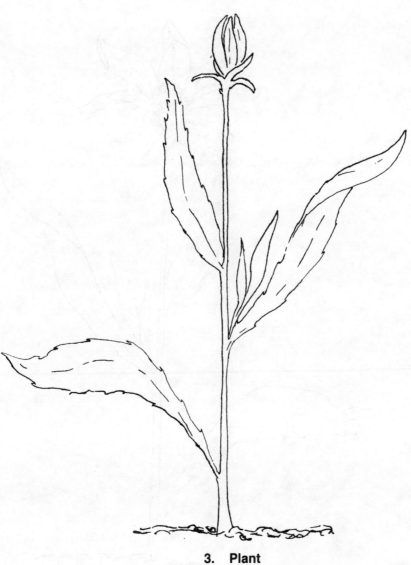

3. **Plant**

4. **Flowering plant**

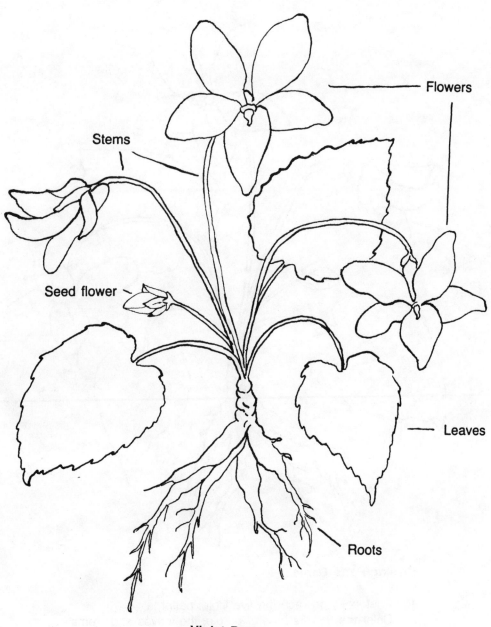

Violet Parts

Missing Parts Game

1. Photocopy or trace the five violet patterns.
2. Color the flowers blue or purple, the leaves and stems green, and the roots brown.
3. Mount on cardboard and laminate.
4. As you hold up each picture have the children tell which part is missing.

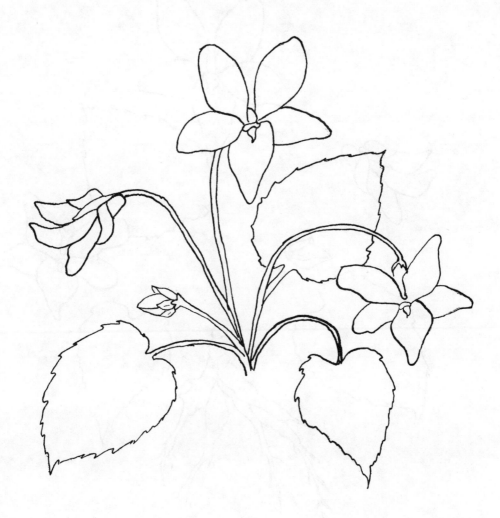

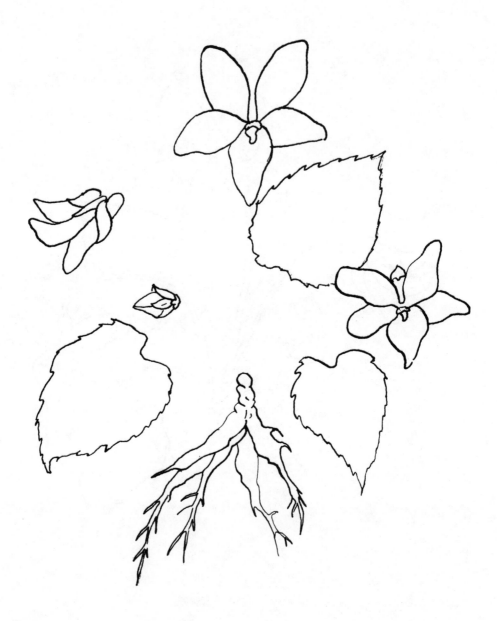

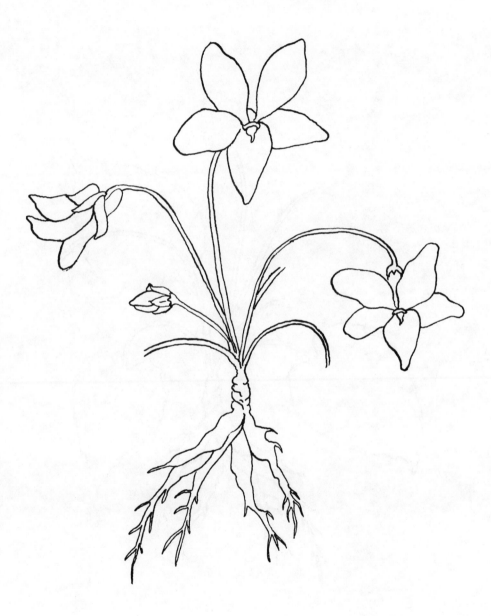

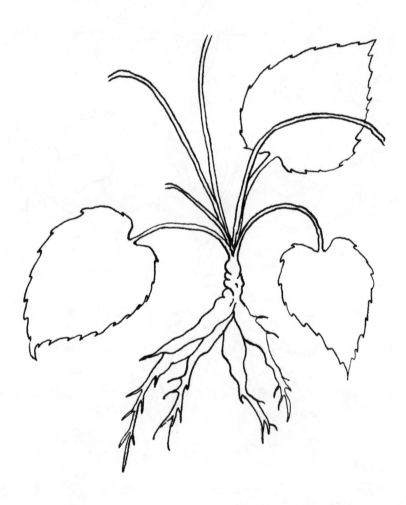

Make violet butter and spread it on crackers. Here's the recipe:

Violet Butter
Wash and shake water from 1½ cups fresh violet blossoms—press down in cup for fairly firm measure.

1½ cups water
3 tablespoons lemon juice
3 cups sugar
1 package "sure-jell"

Place violets, ¾ cup water, and lemon juice in blender. Blend at high speed one minute. Add sugar. Blend another minute. Add "sure-jell" into remaining water. Boil full 2 minutes, stirring constantly. Pour hot mixture into blender—blend 2 minutes. Pour into sterilized, hot jelly jars and seal. When cool, store in freezer. Keeps several months. Makes 3 cups butter or 5 medium jelly glasses.

While eating this treat, look at pictures of animals that eat violets.

White-tailed Deer   **Junco**

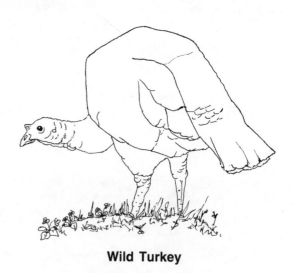

Wild Turkey

Animals That Eat Violets

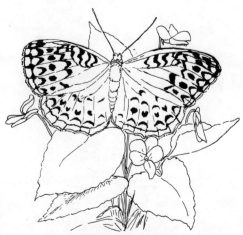

Fritillary Butterfly

Cottontail Rabbit

Mouse

Mourning Dove

Ruffed Grouse

Woodchuck

SUMMER

Body
Awareness

Summer! A time to run, free of coats, mittens, and boots. A time to feel the sun on bare arms and legs. In summer, dance with the flowers, shake hands with the oak, and learn stillness from the pine.

Children enjoy summer with their bodies.

OAK TREES

There are two groups of oaks: white oaks and black oaks. White oaks have leaves with rounded lobes. Their acorns have sweet kernels, and they mature in one year. Black oaks have leaves that end in sharp points. Their acorns have bitter kernels and require two years to mature.

The tree itself requires about a century to mature. The average age of an oak is two hundred to three hundred years. They start to produce acorns at about twenty years of age.

Acorns are good food for animals. These nuts contain protein, vitamins, calcium, and phosphorous; they are also relatively high in fat and carbohydrates. Many birds eat acorns, including blue jays, nuthatches, titmice, ruffed grouse, and wild turkeys. Mammals that eat acorns include chipmunks, mice, flying squirrels, raccoons, and deer. But the greatest acorn consumer is the squirrel. The gray squirrel buries nuts singly and forgets to eat some of them. These then sprout and grow into trees. Many insects also find food and protection within the oak tree.

People also find oaks useful. Native Americans harvested the acorns to grind into flour. The early white settlers used the galls and bark to make ink and dyes. Today the wood is used to make furniture, flooring, and firewood.

My thanks to the Green Witch, Susun Weed, for introducing me to the trees of the thirteen moons. According to the lunar calendar, the oak represents the seventh lunation, which occurs in mid-summer. Oak, the symbol for strength, endurance, and triumph, also serves as the axis to connect earth to heaven.

We can do no better than to start the summer's physical activities with the oak—Strength, Endurance, Triumph!

White Oak

Black Oak

195

LESSON

This lesson is my all-time favorite. It was the first I designed for on-the-road programs, and it is always a hit. I use an oak sapling, but any species will do.

"Today I would like to introduce you to a very special friend of mine. This is Oak. Would you like to shake hands with Oak? You know this tree is a lot like you. Today we will find out exactly how this tree is like you. Can you show me your arms?" Allow time for the children to hold out their arms. Encourage them to answer questions about their arms, such as, "How many arms do you have? What can you do with your arms?" Ask them to stretch as high as they can with their arms . . . to reach for the sun. "This tree has arms too, but we call its arms *branches*. Can you say 'branches'? Let's count the branches. This tree is reaching its branches to the sun."

"Show me your skin." Allow time for children to feel their skin on their hands, their arms, and their faces. "This skin covers you all over and protects you. A tree has skin, too, but we call this skin *bark*. This is the *bark* of this tree. Can you say 'bark'? This bark protects the tree just as your skin protects you."

"I want everyone to stand up. Stand still and look at me. Oh, you are standing so beautifully. Why aren't you falling down? Because your feet keep you from falling over. Show me your feet. See how they keep you standing up straight and tall? This tree has feet, too, but we call these feet *roots*. Here are the *roots* of this tree. Can you say 'roots'? These roots make sure the tree stands up straight so that it doesn't fall over."

"You have arms . . . show me your arms. A tree has arms, and we call those arms [wait for children to respond] *branches*."

"You have skin . . . show me your skin. A tree has skin, and we call that skin [wait for children to respond] *bark*."

"You have feet . . . show me your feet. A tree has feet, and we call these feet [wait for children to respond] *roots*."

"You can move around with your feet. You can walk; you can run; you can jump. But a tree cannot. Its feet, which we call roots, are planted in the ground, so the tree has to stay in one place. Pretend to be trees. Stand straight and tall. Don't move your roots—remember, they are planted in the ground. A wind is coming. Show me how the tree moves in the wind."

Here you may need to give some guidelines: that they must stand in one place; that the wind would move the branches and the body. Have the children move to a gentle breeze, to a brisk wind; show how they would stand on a hot day, on a cold day.

"This tree [point to the sapling] is just a baby oak. Let's go visit its parent." (Go outside and walk to an oak.) "Here is our tree . . . *oak*. Touch its bark with your hands." As you give these instructions, follow them yourself to encourage the children. "Rub the bark with your hands, with your cheek. How does the bark feel?" Allow the children enough time to feel the texture of the bark. Make bark rubbings. Display the rubbings in a prominent place.

Make tree puppets from paper bags. Play the Billy B. songs "This Bark on Me" and "My Roots" (see Resources). Have the children move the tree puppets to the songs. Read *A Tree Is Nice* by Janice May Udry (see Resources) to both children and puppets.

Use a large sheet of newsprint and the flat side of a crayon to create a bark rubbing.

Make leaf prints or leaf rubbings. Collect and press leaves. Play leaf-matching games.

Outside, have each child collect his or her own leaf and then study it. Learn the shape, the color, and the insect holes. Place all the leaves in a pile and see if each child can find his or her own leaf.

Make leaf sun catchers from pressed leaves and clear adhesive plastic. Make a leaf mural. Play a leaf-sorting game—classify by size, shape, and color.

With your collections of acorns, twigs, and leaves, make a feely box. Have the children guess which part of the tree they're feeling.

Visit the outdoor oak again. Join hands around it. How many children does it take to encircle it? How tall is it in comparison to the children. To the school? Ask the children to imitate the shape of the tree with their bodies. Lie on the ground and look through its branches to the sky. Is any other plant growing on it (such as lichen)? Watch the tree to see what animals and insects use it. Note what parts of the tree insects, animals, and birds use. Listen to the tree's sounds.

Oak Tree

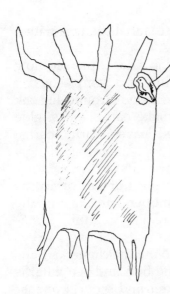

Tree Puppet

1. Cut roots from the open end of a lunch bag.
2. Have children tear strips from other lunch bags and glue onto the top of their bags for twigs.
3. Color trunk brown.
4. Put a bird sticker near the top in branches.

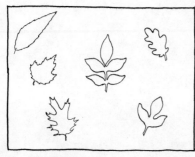

Leaf Matching Game

1. Collect six different leaves and press.
2. Trace leaf shapes onto large poster board and color.
3. Have children match pressed leaves to leaf shapes.

Chart the progress of the tree in its seasonal changes with a picture chart.

Note how people use wood. If you take trips, see how different people stack firewood. Bring in a sample of oak furniture, flooring, and firewood. Scrounge around for oak scraps from a local lumberyard to make oak plaques: glue parts of the oak tree (twigs, pressed leaves, bark, acorns) onto the wood.

Expand your oak lessons into year-round activities.

In autumn, collect acorns. Count the number of acorns collected from one tree. Cut an acorn open and examine the inside; there may be a white grub there. Play counting games with acorns.

In winter, collect a few oak twigs. Note the cluster of buds at the end of the twig. Cut open the bud and see what is inside. Put the bud in a glass of water and see if it opens.

In spring, watch with anticipation as the oaks leaf out.

SQUIRRELS

Cities are home to several mammals, including the gray squirrel. These active animals have adjusted well to city living. Many have learned to look before they cross the street! Squirrels have even made use of man-made structures. They need a feeding lookout—high places from which to feed and watch for enemies. In the city, statues and roofs of buildings serve them well. The lookout will have bits and pieces from the squirrel's meal: scales from cones, shells from nuts. Squirrels have learned that people will feed them in city parks. The gray squirrel population in an old cemetery in the city may be twice as large as in the woods. Trees in these cemeteries are often large and old, and thus produce many nuts.

The word *squirrel* comes from the Greek for "shade tail." And, indeed, these mammals are easily identified by their broad, flat, furry tails. These tails help the squirrel in many ways: as a balancer for its treetop antics; as an umbrella for rain or for shade in the sun; as a rudder when it leaps from tree to tree; as a parachute if the squirrel falls; and as a blanket to cover the squirrel's underside and nose.

Squirrels eat treebark, buds, and seeds. They do not have cheek pouches, so they must carry one nut at a time. Each nut is buried separately in a hole two to three inches deep; each squirrel may bury hundreds of nuts. In winter, they dig them up when food is scarce. But they do not find all of them, so the unclaimed food germinates and grows into trees.

Squirrels make several noises: barking, chattering, scolding, and squeaking.

The squirrel has short legs, which are more suitable for

climbing than running. It uses its front paws to wash its face and to hold food to its mouth. It has two pairs of gnawing teeth that grow continuously, so the squirrel must keep gnawing at things to trim and sharpen these teeth.

Gray squirrels prefer to nest in holes, but if one is unavailable, they'll make an open leaf-and-twig nest in some branches. These nests are lined with soft grasses. The young are usually born in the summer. There are three to five babies in a litter. They are born blind and naked. At six weeks, however, they are fully furred and ready to leave the nest. A young squirrel spends its time playing. It runs along branches, making longer and longer jumps. This play is serious business, for the squirrel is learning how to keep its balance and how not to fall when jumping.

LESSON

The Squirrel's Tail

The leaves are turning,
the day is cool.
See all the children
walking to school.

High up in a tree
on an oak branch
Is a gray squirrel
doing her dance.
Her tail helps her balance
so she won't fall.

She runs, jumps, and plays
on treetops so tall.
All of a sudden
it starts to rain.
Up goes her tail
so she won't complain.

The rain is over,
the sun returns
She keeps her tail up
so she won't burn.
Squirrel jumps too far,
down, down, she goes.

Up goes her parachute tail,
so she won't bang her nose.
She climbs up a tree
and gathers some leaves.
Busily she works
as her nest she weaves.

It's time for a nap,
she gives a big yawn.
Her fluffy gray tail
keeps her cozy and warm.

Squirrel

As you read this poem to the children, encourage them to make hand motions to accompany it.

Outdoors, you say, "Today you are squirrels. You will do some things a squirrel does. A squirrel has to walk very carefully on the branches so it won't fall off." Have the children walk on ramps, on pieces of rope stretched along the ground, or on balance beams while pretending they are squirrels in the treetops. They can climb a jungle gym or swingset ladder while pretending they are squirrels climbing a tree. "I am a dog. You must run to [specify a location] so I can't catch you. Squirrels run fast!"

Give each child an acorn. "Now you are a squirrel who wants to save its acorn for winter. Find a place to bury your acorn."

"Now the squirrel is tired. Crawl into a ball and go to sleep."

Do "The Squirrel" finger play from Marc Brown's *Finger Rhymes* with the children (see Resources).

Play acorn beanbag toss. An old box can serve as the hole in the oak tree. "Acorns" are made from brown material and filled with dry white beans. Toss the acorns into the tree.

Dress the squirrel tree.

Using duplicate copies of magazines, cut out pairs of squirrel pictures. Mount them on poster board in random fashion. The children can match pictures that are alike.

Let the children examine and eat various nuts. Place nuts or sunflower seeds out for the squirrels. Watch how they eat. Watch to see if they will dig little holes to bury acorns.

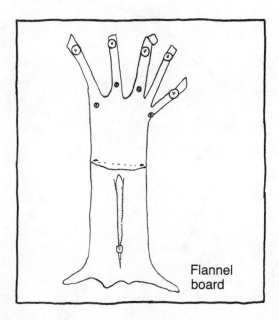

Flannel
board

Squirrel Tree

1. Cut tree shape from brown felt in two pieces. Sew together on edges.
2. In bottom half cut slit large enough for 6–7 inch zipper. Sew zipper in.
3. Sew buttons on branches.
4. Sew snaps on branches and trunk.
5. Have children "dress" the tree.

Patterns for Squirrel Tree (see pages 206–207)

1. Cut one mother squirrel. Cut slits in middle, thread shoelace through slits for children to tie.
2. Cut numerous leaves in yellow, red, orange felt.
3. Cut slit in leaves and button onto tree.
4. Cut two or three baby squirrels, place in tree through zipper.
5. Cut three or four brown acorns, sew on snaps to snap onto tree.

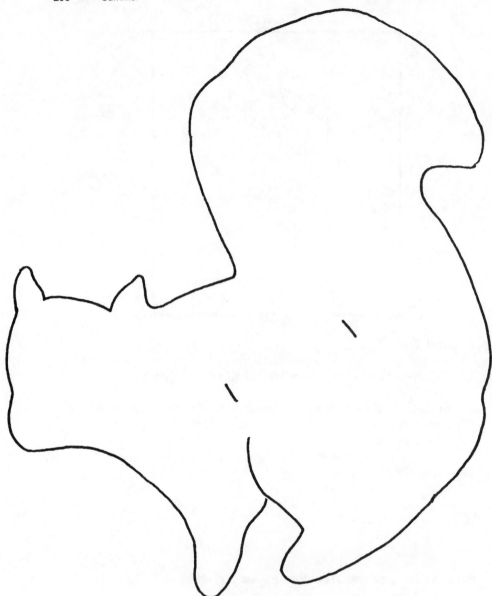

Mother Squirrel Pattern

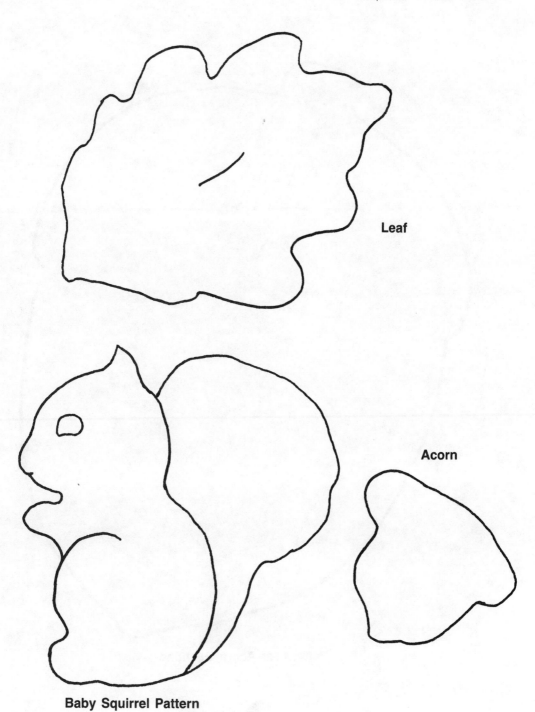

Leaf

Acorn

Baby Squirrel Pattern

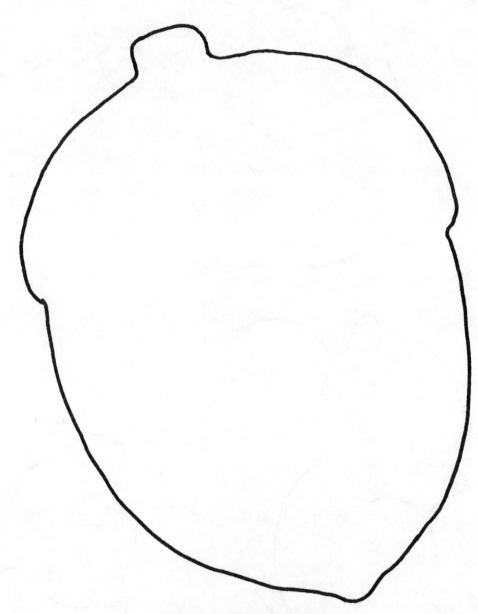

Pattern for Acorn Beanbag

WHITE PINE

Just as princess pine and turtles are determined survivors of an ancient past, so is the pine tree. Its moisture-proof foliage has helped it to survive countless snowy winters. This foliage consists of slender needles. The white pine sports a five-needle bundle. Each bundle juts out from the tips of the twigs, creating an overall airy effect. As the wind blows, the needles vibrate and whisper. Ask the children to tell you what the white pine says.

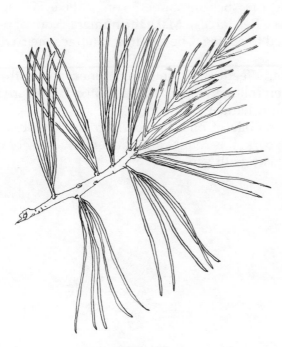

White Pine

LESSON

Body awareness consists not only of movement, but also of stillness. Stillness, however, is not an overwhelming characteristic of young children. One activity to develop this ability is to have the children lie under a white pine and look up through the branches. Speak softly about what they see. Have them close their eyes and listen. Listen to the stories the white pine tells.

When the children get up, examine the five-needle bundle. "Here is a branch from a white pine tree. And here are its leaves. We call this kind of leaves *needles*. Feel them and tell me why we call them needles." Let children feel them until one child says that the needles are pointed or sharp, or long and thin. "In each group there are five needles. Let's count them. One-two-three-four-five! That's how we know it is a white pine tree. A white pine has five needles in each group." Count five fingers. Have individual children bring five pinecones to you. Count out loud, "one-two-three-four-five!" Sing the "Sesame Street" song, "Five People in My Family" (see Resources). Make the numeral 5 out of pinecone scales glued to oaktag. The children can trace the 5 with their fingers.

Make bird feeders by smearing pinecones with peanut butter, then rolling them in birdseed mix. Loop yarn around the top for a hanger.

Make a mobile of pine tree bark, cones, and branches.

Feel the bark; it is rough, and, depending on the weather, may be sticky with sap.

BOX TURTLES

Are your students fascinated by dinosaurs? No, you can't take a field trip to spot dinosaurs, but you can follow up your dinosaur unit by learning about the remnants of that long-ago time that exist today. Dragonflies, princess pine, white pine trees, and turtles all have ancestors, which existed even before the age of dinosaurs.

Turtles are reptiles whose ancestors date back some 200 million years. Reptiles all share certain characteristics: they are cold blooded; they have lungs, which breathe air; their skin is covered with scales or plates; and they lay eggs. The most identifying characteristic of turtles is the shell. The upper part is called the *carapace*; the lower shell is called the *plastron*. The hinged plastron of the box turtle allows it to enclose itself completely for protection.

The male box turtle's eyes have orange-red irises. Box turtles have no external ear parts. They have poor hearing but can detect vibrations through their shells. The mouth is a hooked beak with horny edges; they have no teeth. Box

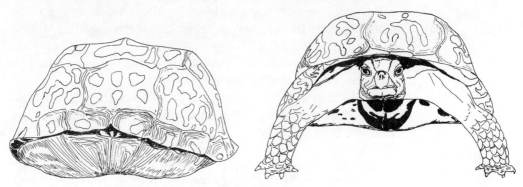

Box Turtle

turtles eat berries, slugs, snails, insects, earthworms, and mushrooms.

In early summer, the female box turtle buries four to five round white eggs in a sunny spot. They hatch in about three months. The young may hibernate soon after without eating. At age five, they mate and lay eggs. At age twenty, they are fully grown. They may live to be eighty years old.

LESSON

Introduce the subject of turtles with the old favorite finger play by Vachel Lindsay, "The Little Turtle" (see Resources).

You can use any turtle for this lesson. We borrowed box turtles from a local zoo. If you can find a turtle near your school or nature center, enjoy it for the day and then release it exactly where you found it. Turtles do not like to be away from home. Allow the children to watch the turtle move. Have the children feel the carapace. Encourage discussion by pointing out the distinguishing body parts. Be sure children wash their hands after handling the turtle. Although a rare occurrence, turtles can carry salmonella bacteria.

Make turtle-shell paper bags as described by Edith Sisson in her book, *Nature with Children of All Ages* (see Resources): "Cut a hole in the bottom of the bag large enough for a child's head to go through; on each side of the bag near the bottom, cut holes for the arms. Have the child color one side of the bag to look like a turtle's top shell, the carapace, and the other side to look like the bottom shell, the plastron."[*]

Put the bags on the children; let them walk and act like turtles. Recite the Lindsay finger-play poem together, acting it out. As the children move around, they will begin to recognize the advantage of the shell (protection) as well as its limitation (restricted movement).

Read Frank Asch's *Turtle Tales* (see Resources) to the children. Maybe you'll want to act out the Aesop fable, "The Tortoise and the Hare."

*From *Nature with Children of All Ages* by Edith A. Sisson, The Massachusetts Audubon Society © 1982, reprinted by permission of the publisher, Prentice-Hall, Inc., Englewood Cliffs, N.J.

PIGEONS

Pigeons came to North America with the colonists as farm animals. Gradually many of these birds escaped from the farms and moved to the cities. They adapted well to city life, nesting on window ledges, statues, and towers. Pigeons exhibit "street smarts": they will take food from people, yet scurry away when threatened. They seem to thrive on dodging traffic and young children.

Young children are fascinated with pigeons. One day I watched a small boy walk along behind a pigeon, imitating it exactly—one foot in front of the other, heads bobbing in unison as pigeon and boy walked.

They are also pesky. There is a pair nesting over the door to the library where I work. Every morning I scoop up the twigs that have fallen from the nest. The male is responsible for my chore, as he is the one who finds the right nesting place. He sits on this chosen spot and coos. The nest itself is made from stiff twigs, which the male brings to the female. She takes this material and builds a rather sloppy nest. Both birds set on the eggs, which hatch in seventeen days.

The baby pigeons, called squabs, are fed "pigeon milk." This substance is white in color and is similar to milk. When the pigeons start setting on the eggs, special changes take place in their crops. By the time the eggs hatch, the crop is ready to produce this pigeon milk.

As the days go by, pieces of food are added to the pigeon milk. After about three weeks, the squabs are ready to be on their own.

A pair of pigeons can raise several broods a year. The average lifespan of a pigeon is fifteen years. All of this adds up to a lot of pigeons in our cities!

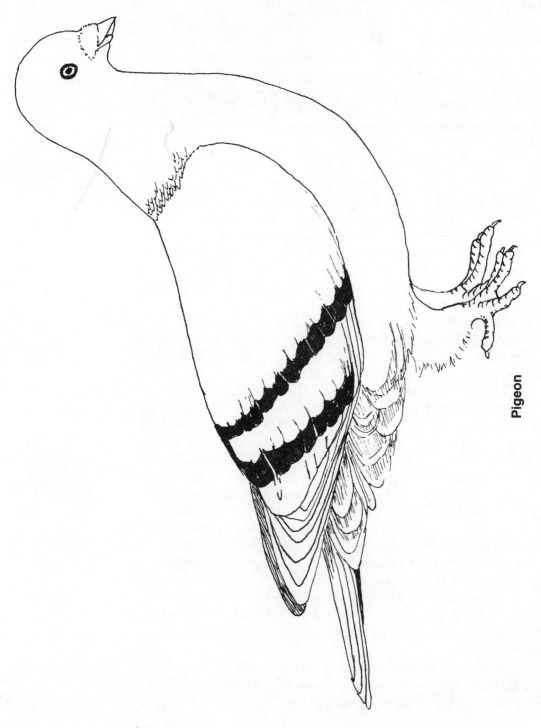

Pigeon

LESSON

Using this illustration, discuss the various body parts of the pigeon. Discuss the function of each body part. Note the pigeon's three toes; compare them to the five toes of the human. Allow time for conversation and experimentation: "What do we do with our feet?" Walk, run, and stand. Have the children walk like pigeons.

Discuss how the male pigeon collects twigs for the nest. Put a sheet of plastic in the center of the playground. Place straws on top of the plastic. Have the children stand about twenty feet away from the plastic and ask them to walk like pigeons to the plastic. Encourage them to fold their arms up and place their hands in their armpits to simulate wings. When they get to the plastic, have the children pick up the straw with their "beaks" and then pigeon-walk back to the starting place. When all the straws are at the starting place, arrange them in a loosely constructed nest. Time to sleep: have the children stand like pigeons, with heads tucked under wings.

Eat like pigeons, snacking on bits of bread or popcorn.

Act out "Mrs. Peck-Pigeon" (see Resources).

Pigeon watching depends, of course, on the availability of pigeons. If there are not any near your school, try walking to the closest park. When you see them, try these activities: feed them bread crumbs and watch how they eat them; listen to the sounds that pigeons make; watch them walk and fly; note their colors and the placement of their body parts. Watch them fly, roost, dodge traffic, and avoid people's feet.

FLOWERS

The three-year-old asks, "Why do plants have flowers?" The clearest explanation to be found lies in Ruth Heller's picture book, *The Reason for a Flower* (see Resources). Oh, the answer? To manufacture seeds.

Children love flowers indiscriminately. Witness the bouquets of dandelions they present to teachers every spring!

LESSON

Strumming an autoharp, sing "Summer is a-Comin' " to the old tune, "Train is a-Comin' ":

> *Summer is a-comin', oh yeah*
> *Summer is a-comin', oh yeah*
> *Summer is a-comin'*
> *Summer is a-comin'*
> *Summer is a-comin'*
> *Oh yeah!*
>
> *Flowers are bloomin', oh yeah*
> *Flowers are bloomin', oh yeah*
> *Flowers are bloomin'*
> *Flowers are bloomin'*
> *Flowers are bloomin'*
> *Oh yeah!*

Then say, "Summer is a magical time of year. Plants grow up, up [demonstrate with body]. Leaves sprout—and flowers blossom!" At this point, flowers magically cascade from

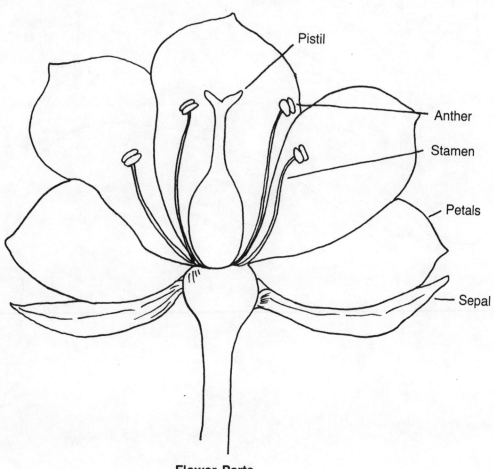

Pistil

Anther

Stamen

Petals

Sepal

Flower Parts

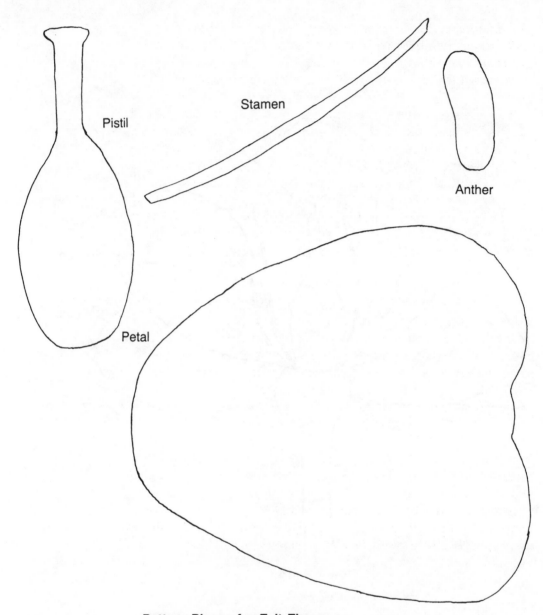

Pistil

Stamen

Anther

Petal

Pattern Pieces for Felt Flower

1. These pieces may also be used for "Pin the Anther on the Stamen."
2. Cut out one pistil.
3. Cut out a number of petals, stamens, and anthers.

your fingertips, to the utter amazement of the children. (This nifty flower trick may be purchased at most magic stores for less than $5.00.)

Using felt pieces on a flannel board, name the parts of the flower.

Play pin-the-anther-on-the-stamen, just as you play pin-the-tail-on-the-donkey. See the illustration on page 218.

Make giant tulips out of construction paper. Place them around the playground. Give directions: "Run to the red tulip. Hop to the yellow tulip. Walk backwards to the purple tulip."

Rearrange the giant tulips into a large circle, with one tulip for each child. Play a variant of musical chairs: when the music stops, the children must land on a tulip.

Now is the time when you are glad that the seed companies filled your mailbox with multiple copies of their catalogues. Cut out pairs of flower pictures from duplicate copies. Arrange them on poster board and cover them with clear adhesive plastic. Have the children find the matching pairs. Cut out large photographs of flowers. Glue them to construction paper. Cut each flower in half and mix up the halves. Have the children put the correct flowers together.

Cut out and mount pictures of flowers. Have the children arrange them by color, with all the yellows in one pile, and so on.

Be sure to take the opportunity to find flowers on your trips outside. Walk around the neighborhood and note the planted flowers. Also, look for the wildflowers growing in vacant lots and along sidewalks. Compare and contrast the locations where different flowers grow, their colors, and their smells. Use a hand lens to examine them closely.

QUEEN ANNE'S LACE

In summer, Grandma Mary would make bouquets of multi-colored Queen Anne's lace. No, it doesn't come that way; the blossoms are white. I'll reveal her secret later.

Queen Anne's lace is a weed found in vacant city lots as well as along roadsides. The airy, delicate blossoms resemble lace, which Queen Anne of England wore on her dresses. The tiny blossoms form flower clusters. These are elegantly arranged around a larger cluster. In the center of this larger cluster there is often a dark purple blossom. Anna Comstock wrote:

> The reason for this giant floret at the center of the wide, circular flower-cluster is a mystery; and so far as I know, the botanists have not yet explained the reason for its presence. May we not, then, be at liberty to explain its origin on the supposition that her Royal Highness, Queen Anne, was wont to fasten her lace medallions upon her royal person with garnet-headed pins?

Each set of flower clusters is called an umbel. As the flowers wither, the umbel turns inward, forming a little brown cup or "bird's nest." Within each cup are scores of little spiny seeds (see page 35 for more information on autumn seed dispersal).

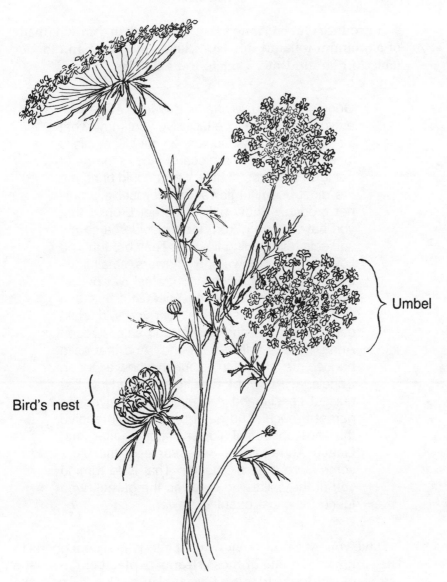

Umbel

Bird's nest

Queen Anne's Lace

LESSON

To introduce Queen Anne's lace, I dress up in a crown (made of aluminum foil and flower stickers) and wrap an old lacy tablecloth around me. I relate the following tale:

> Good day to you. My name is Queen Anne and, as you can see, I love lace. Do you know what lace is? [Most preschoolers do not.] See, this is lace. [Pass around a piece of lace.] One day I put forth a decree: that whoever could bring me the most beautiful flower would receive a garnet brooch. [Show a fake garnet brooch that you have made.] From far and wide came my subjects, all bringing flowers. They brought red flowers, yellow flowers, big flowers, small flowers—all kinds of flowers. But alas! Not one of them did I consider the most beautiful. Just as I was about to despair, a four-year-old child came up to me and bowed and said, 'Queen Anne, here is a flower I found.' And that child handed me this! [With a flourish, show a Queen Anne's lace flower.] 'Oh, How lovely! How Exquisite!' I exclaimed. And that child received the garnet brooch. And each of you shall receive the most beautiful flower, named after me: Queen Anne's lace! See—some of the blossoms have a purple center. That is to remind you of the child who received the garnet, who found the most beautiful flower.

Have you ever noticed how hot it gets *after* school opens in late summer? On one of those steamy September days, take the class outdoors to pick Queen Anne's lace. Bring the blossoms indoors and put them in glasses of water to which food coloring has been added. (This is Grandma Mary's secret.) After a day or two see the delicate pastel shades as these flowers "drink" the colored water.

Press some of the blossoms in a flower press. When they are dried, use them to make rubbings. (See page 197 for instructions on how to do this.)

On a day when the children have excess energy, take them outside to dig up a Queen Anne's lace plant. The long taproot goes deep into the earth, searching for nutrients. It will take a lot of effort to dig it out! Engage in this dramatic play:

Become a Queen Anne's lace plant. Close your eyes. Plant your long taproot deep into the ground. Into the earth it grows—past stones, past worms—down, down, down. . . . You are now deeply rooted. Slowly, above the ground, the stalk goes up, up. Frilly leaves sprout. Up, up, up, you grow.

Lacy white flowers bloom from your fingertips, from your head. You open up the blossom wide and flat to catch the warmth of the sun. Insects come to you to collect nectar. You enjoy their company. Oops! Here comes a rainstorm. You hang your blossoms down so you don't lose your pollen. The sun comes back and you lift your blossoms to the sun. You sit and smile in the sun.

Summer is going by. Nights are getting cooler. Your white blossoms turn brown. They curl toward the center. Can you curl your fingers? They curl into the center to protect the little seeds inside. Oh! A dog just pushed against you. You giggle because some of your seeds stuck to the dog! You know that somewhere he'll shake them off and new Queen Anne's lace plants will grow. And that makes you happy.

Have the children deck themselves with Queen Anne's lace and dance. I especially like to use "Bergamasca," the fourth Movement of Suite no. 2 of Ottorino Respighi's *Ancient Airs and Dances* as an accompaniment. I am listening now to this lilting melody, imagining you and your children dancing joyously with nature.

Resources

Preface

Pg. iv   Comstock, Anna. *Handbook of Nature Study.* Ithaca, NY: Cornell University Press, 1911.

Pg. viii   Watson, Nancy Dingman. *Blueberries Lavender: Songs of the Farmer's Children.* Reading, Mass.: Addison-Wesley, 1977.

Introduction

Pg. 4   Traditional American folk tune "Oats, Peas, Beans and Barley Grow" may be found in many folksong books, including Winn, Marie, ed. *The Fireside Book of Children's Songs.* New York: Simon and Schuster, 1966.

Pg. 4   Raffi. *The Second Raffi Songbook.* New York: Crown Publishers, 1986.

Pg. 6   National Wildlife Federation publishes *Ranger Rick* and *Your Big Backyard.* Write to 1412 16th St., Washington, D.C. 20036.

Pg. 6   The Young Naturalist Foundation publishes *Owl and Chickadee.* Write to P.O. Box 11314, Des Moines, IA 50340.

Pg. 7   For hand lenses, write for catalog from Museum Products, Gold Star Highway, Mystic, CT.

Autumn

Pg. 10   Teale, Edwin Way. *Autumn Across America.* New York: Dodd, Mead, 1981.

Pp. 14, 16   Raposo, Joe, and Jeffrey Moss. "The People in Your Neighborhood." *The Sesame Street Song Book.* New York: Simon and Schuster, 1971.

Pp. 23, 25   Raposo, Joe, and Jeffrey Moss. "Up and Down." *The Sesame Street Song Book.* New York: Simon and Schuster, 1971.

Pg. 30   Write to the American Rabbit Breeders Association, c/o Glenn Carr, P.O. Box 426, Bloomington, IL 61702 for a list of rabbit breeders near you.

Pg. 32   Bartoli, Jennifer. *In a Meadow, Two Hares Hide.* Chicago: Albert Whitman & Company, 1978.

Pg. 35   Peterson, Roger Tory. *A Field Guide to Wildflowers of Northeastern and North Central North America.* Boston: Houghton Mifflin, 1968.

Pg. 42   Corbo, Margaret S., and Diane M. Barras. *Arnie the Darling Starling.* Boston: Houghton Mifflin, 1983.

Pg. 43   Winn, Marie, ed. "Bluebird." *The Fireside Book of Children's Songs.* New York: Simon and Schuster, 1966.

Pg. 45   Graham, Ada. *Six Little Chickadees: A Scientist and Her Work with Birds.* New York: Four Winds Press, 1982.

Pg. 49   Hart, Jane. "Five Little Chickadees." *Singing Bee: A Collection of Favorite Children's Songs.* New York: Lothrup, Lee and Shepard Books, 1982.

Pg. 49   Hawkinson, Lucy Ozone, and John Hawkinson. *Winter Tree Birds.* Chicago: Albert Whitman & Company, 1971.

Pg. 49   Wolff, Ashley. *A Year of Birds.* New York: Dodd, Mead, 1984.

Pg. 52   O'Neill, Eugene. "Desire Under the Elms." *Nine Plays.* New York: Random House, 1954.

Pg. 53   Kumin, Maxine. "Stones." *Up Country: Poems of New England.* New York: Harper & Row, 1972.

Pg. 56   Ross, George Maxim. *What Did the Rock Say?* New York: Random House, 1970.

Pg. 58   Lionni, Leo. *Frederick.* New York: Pantheon, 1967.

Winter

Pg. 63   O'Neill, Mary. *Hailstones and Halibut Bones.* New York: Doubleday, 1961.

Pg. 71   Bentley, W. A., and W. J. Humphreys. *Snow Crystals.* New York: Dover Publications, 1962.

Pg. 72   Dickinson, Emily. "The sky is low—the clouds are mean. . . ." *American Poetry and Prose.* Norman Foerster, ed. Boston: Houghton Mifflin, 1957.

Pg. 72   Wegen, Ron. *Sky Dragon.* New York: Greenwillow Books, 1982.

Pg. 73   Winston, George. "Snow." *Piano Solos.* California: Windham Hill Records, 1982.

Pg. 73   Whittier, John Greenleaf. "Snow-Bound: A Winter Idyl." *American Poetry and Prose.* Norman Foerster, ed. Boston: Houghton Mifflin, 1957.

Pg. 79   O'Neill, Mary. *Hailstones and Halibut Bones.* New York: Doubleday, 1961.

Pg. 79   Teale, Edwin Way. *Wandering Through Winter.* New York: Dodd, Mead, 1957.

Pg. 87   Museum Products, Gold Star Highway, Mystic, CT.

Pg. 90   Rombauer, Irma S., and Marion Rombauer Becker. *Joy of Cooking.* Indiana: Bobbs-Merrill, 1964.

Pg. 95   Stevenson, Robert Louis. "My Shadow." *Robert Louis Stevenson's A Child's Garden of Verses.* New York: Golden Press, 1978.

Pg. 99   Raposo, Joe, and Jeffrey Moss. "Bein' Green." *The Sesame Street Song Book.* New York: Simon and Schuster, 1971.

Pg. 99   O'Neill, Mary. *Hailstones and Halibut Bones.* New York: Doubleday, 1961.

Pg. 111   Burgess, Thornton W. *The Burgess Flower Book for Children.* Boston: Little Brown, 1928.

Pg. 117   Prisms may be purchased from Museum Products, Gold Star Highway, Mystic, CT.

Pg. 117   Freeman, Don. *A Rainbow of My Own.* New York: Viking, 1966.

Pg. 117   Frank, Marjorie. *I Can Make A Rainbow: Things to Create and Do . . . For Children and Their Grown Up Friends.* Tennessee: Incentive Publications, 1976.

Spring

Pg. 120   McQuilkin, Rennie. "Skunk Cabbage."

Pg. 131   Write or call the American Dairy Goat Association, P.O. Box 865, Spindale, NC 28160, (704) 286-3801, for information about dairy goats.

Pg. 132   Carroll, Ricki and Robert. *Cheesemaking Made Easy,* Vermont: Garden Way Publishing, 1982.

Pg. 145   Kilham, Lawrence and Peter. "The Frog Pond." Rhode Island: Droll Yankees, Inc., 1969.

Pg. 145   Write or call Carolina Biological Supply Company, 2700 York Road, Burlington, NC 27218, (919) 584-0381, for information about obtaining live frogs.

Pg. 151   Conover, Chris. "Froggie Went a-Courting." New York: Farrar Straus Giroux, 1986.

Pg. 156   Heller, Ruth. *Chickens Aren't the Only Ones.* New York: Putnam Publishing Group, 1981.

Pg. 168   Carle, Eric. *The Very Hungry Caterpillar.* New York: Putnam Publishing Group, 1981.

Pg. 178   Raffi. *The Second Raffi Songbook.* New York: Crown Publishers, 1986.

Pg. 151   Lobel, Arnold. "The Garden." *Frog and Toad Together.*
179   New York: Harper & Row, 1972.

Pg. 179   Billy B. "I Am a Sprout." *Billy B. Sings About Trees.* Wisconsin: Do Dreams Music, 1978.

Summer

Pg. 197   Billy B. "This Bark on Me" and "My Roots." *Billy B. Sings About Trees.* Wisconsin: Do Dreams Music, 1978.

Pg. 197   Udry, Janice May. *A Tree Is Nice.* New York: Harper & Row, 1956.

Pg. 204   Brown, Marc. "The Squirrel." *Finger Rhymes.* New York: Dutton, 1980.

Pg. 210   Raposo, Joe, and Jeffrey Moss. "Five People in My Family." *The Sesame Street Song Book.* New York: Simon and Schuster, 1971.

Pg. 212   Lindsay, Vachel. "The Little Turtle." *Finger Rhymes,* New York: Dutton, 1980.

Pg. 212   Sisson, Edith A. *Nature with Children of All Ages: Activities and Adventures for Exploring, Learning and Enjoying the World Around Us.* Englewood Cliffs, NJ: Prentice-Hall, 1982.

Pg. 212   Asch, Frank. *Turtle Tales,* New York: Dial Press, 1978.

Pg. 215   Farjeon, Eleanor. "Mrs. Peck-Pigeon." *Animal Poems for Children.* DeWitt Conyers, ed. New York: Golden Press, 1982.

Pg. 216   Heller, Ruth. *The Reason for a Flower,* New York: Grosset & Dunlap, 1983.

Pg. 220   Comstock, Anna, *Handbook of Nature Study,* Ithaca, NY: Cornell University Press, 1911.

Pg. 224   Respighi, Ottorino. "Bergamasca." *Ancient Airs and Dances.*

Index

Page numbers for illustrations are shown in boldface type.